To:

_____

From:

_____

SLEEPLESS NIGHTS *and* KISSES *for* BREAKFAST

SLEEPLESS NIGHTS *and* KISSES *for* BREAKFAST

~

Reflections on Fatherhood

BY MATTEO BUSSOLA

TRANSLATED BY JAMIE RICHARDS

A TarcherPerigee Book

tarcherperigee

An imprint of Penguin Random House LLC
375 Hudson Street
New York, New York 10014

First published in Italy by Einaudi Stile Libero, 2016

Most TarcherPerigee books are available at special quantity discounts for bulk
purchase for sales promotions, premiums, fund-raising, and educational needs.
Special books or book excerpts also can be created to fit specific needs. For
details, write: SpecialMarkets@penguinrandomhouse.com.

ISBN 9780143131373

Printed in the United States of America
1 3 5 7 9 10 8 6 4 2

Book design by Sabrina Bowers
Interior illustrations by Sandra Chiu

Penguin is committed to publishing works of quality and integrity. In that
spirit, we are proud to offer this book to our readers; however, the story, the
experiences, and the words are the author's alone.

to them

Contents

SPRING

SUMMER

FALL

Introduction

My job is being a father. My profession is drawing comics. I write for fun.

I learned the comics profession by drawing, the job of fatherhood by being a father. I had three wonderful teachers: my daughters who are eight, four, and two. Writing, in a sense, was always there.

I decided to put all these things together here, to draw a picture in words alone.

This book is a journal of sorts. It gathers stories, reports, reflections, and near-daily snapshots of my daughters' growth—and my growth through theirs. It's about how being a father has made me a better man, a more confident artist, and a more attentive partner. Also a more tired partner, but it's a shared tiredness, that long-standing fatigue that comes from trying to plan and build something with another person.

Virginia, Ginevra, and Melania are the lens through which I observe the world. The view they provide gives me a different way of looking at everything, even at what I was before they came along. I think this is what's called putting things in perspective. Perspective teaches us to create horizons and to realize that things change depending on how you choose to look at them; that sometimes the future that seems least likely is the result of a leap you started to take before even knowing it. You just have to conquer your fear of leaping when the time comes. Fatherhood was my leap.

Something I've discovered is that the nature of my fears has changed over the years. Having children shifts the nucleus of your fears to a darker place, but at the same time makes it invaluable, a beacon that lights your path instead of a fire that burns your skin. Fears are no longer something to defend against, but to nourish. And it's a job you do in the dark with your eyes perpetually open, almost as if too much life keeps you from closing them and leaves you sleepless forever.

In my sleepless life, I am father, son, friend, cook, guitar player, gardener, illustrator, lover, dishwasher, builder of toy towers, and a ton of other things, every day, and not always in that order. But I've discovered that my role as father is the only one that contains me fully.

Every day I learn from it and every lesson I learn nourishes all the other lessons. My daughters nourish me and remind me that being a father means living in

that gray area between responsibility and careless-
ness, strength and softness. And that goes for everything.

The rest is what follows.

WINTER

The Elephant's Weight

t was January 2007, a Saturday just like today. The sky was low and full of clouds.

I was at the hospital. Seeing the doctors go by, the women in robes, the coffee machines, and the fact that I was about to become a father for the first time made me feel like I wasn't myself, like I was watching someone else's life.

It was nighttime, I was in the waiting room, and I saw no one smoking. "People always smoke in the movies," I thought. But I don't. That also added to my perception of the whole scene as unreal, in slow motion, through a filter.

That filter was me. It was my old conception of myself, my old life, my old idea of everything, everything that was about to change, looming overhead like the puckered clouds outside.

Paola was calm, whereas I was like a drunk one glass short of too many. I went around in a haze, with unsteady feet and an idiotic smile that, seen from the outside, must have made me look relaxed to the point of either unconsciousness or mental impairment.

First, the nurse said eight, then nine, then ten, then eleven, then it stopped making any difference.

It was a long night, interminable—in which I faced all my fears at once and all my powerlessness at once; first all the anxiety and then the adrenaline crash, releasing a joy that had been held under pressure and almost rabidly pervaded my senses.

And so now, as I'm writing this, I realize that in reality I don't want to describe the situation, the terror, the strength I saw and experienced. Because it's not possible or because I don't know the right way to say it. And also because these things are so personal and different for everybody; therefore, my experience would ultimately remain just that: mine.

What I actually want to say—which is also the reason behind this journal, which I'm typing quickly on my iPad while the girls are getting ready for school—is that, in my opinion, there are two decisive moments in a man's life: there's the before, and there's the after.

The before and after aren't the same for everyone. I know people for whom the after was a breakup, others for whom it was getting married. For some it was finding their dream job, for some others it was finding a job at all. For others, the after was going to Haiti with Doctors Without Borders. Once I talked to this old man who I kept just wanting to hug, and he told me what it was like after being liberated by the Americans, and how there are things that cancel out every after and blur lots of befores, that change your future forever right before your eyes.

When you become a father, your after weighs about seven and a half pounds. You can tell even from the first second that this will be a definitive after, the only thing in your life there's no turning back from. Not even if you wanted to, not even if you tried your hardest—no matter what you do with your future, that after will never change.

In return, it will change you. It's already changing you; it already has, in a way you don't know how to articulate but feel in your arms and your legs—a metamorphosis.

In terms of pounds, now I've got about a hundred more. Every day I lug them to school and everywhere else I go. I move like an elephant when I used to move like a gazelle.

But the point is that the gazelle wakes up in the morning because it knows the lion is there. And the lion wakes up every morning because it knows the gazelle is there.

But an elephant couldn't care less. He doesn't run and doesn't hunt. He wakes up after sleeping for a couple hours and does what he needs to do, knowing that it's precisely his being an elephant that keeps it all together. He wakes up when he needs to and moves slowly, even in a china shop.

But when he moves, it's neither for a lion nor a gazelle.

He moves because his life began when he became an elephant. It began *after*. And *that* after, the elephant's after, is the only after in the world that is also a before. It's the ultimate before, the before everything, the beginning and the ending at the same time. It's actually the only experience that cancels out every before and after and transforms everything into a *while*.

An elephant lives only in the present and knows that his present has a certain weight; he feels it in his arms and legs. In his back.

Therein lies his strength. All the strength he needs.

The kind gazelles wish they had and lions can only dream of.

Why Kids Have to
Go to School

I'm in the car, taking Ginevra and Melania to nursery school after taking Virginia to catch the bus for elementary school.

"Dad, why do kids have to go to school?"

"Eh, Ginevra, because they have to."

"But why do kids *have* to go to school though?"

"Because it's their job. Mommies' and daddies' job is to work. Kids' job is going to school."

"But if kids have a job, then why don't we get any money?"

"Oh, you do get money, you know! You bet you do. It just that we daddies and mommies save it for you. Then when you get older, we give it to you."

"How much do we get, Daddy?"

"Hmm, quite a bit. Especially kids who behave at school."

"Like more than a euro?"

"Um, yes, yes, a lot more."

"How much more?"

"Ten euros."

"TEN EUROS? That's a lot!"

"Yep."

"Daddy, when we get back home, will you show me my money?"

I think, "Thank God I didn't say five hundred."

"Sure, Ginevra. I'll show you today when you get home."

"But Daddy, do you get paid for your job too?"

"Well, of course."

"Do you get ten euros too?"

"No, no, I get more. Because I'm a grown-up."

"How much?"

"Twenty euros."

"TWENTY EUROS? Then you have a ton of money! You're rich!"

"No, Ginevra, twenty euros isn't that much money."

"But you're rich, right?"

I look at her in the rearview mirror. I see her eyes laughing. Beside her, Melania is sucking on a sock.

"Of course."

Kids' Party

Paola's away for work, the two little ones are at Grandma and Grandpa's, and Virginia and I are home alone.

Yesterday I took her to one of those horrible elementary school birthday parties. It was held in the Sunday school basement, which the priest was kind enough to let them use, and the atmosphere was straight out of *Nightmare on Elm Street*. The ceilings were barely six feet high, there were tiny slits for windows, a few sad streamers on the walls, and a crooked banner that said "HAPPY BIRTHDAY MAR A NA," since the kids had already pulled down some of the letters. The mothers were all huddled in the back corner next to the potato chips and corn puffs, like so many hens in battery cages.

When we went in, since I was the only dad there, they eyed me as if a drunk, naked Hun had crashed their Christmas portrait session. But it lasted only a second, because moms like me.

After about three minutes Maria Carla was talking

to me about her stiff neck; Mattia's mom was telling me I look like that guy, what's-his-name, you know who I mean, come on; and the birthday girl's mother had brought me a salami sandwich.

All I wanted was to die, and in fact, I stubbornly kept my coat fully zipped and my scarf on, as the international sign for, "I'm just dropping her off and coming to pick her up later; don't get any ideas, my getaway car's out front with the motor running and a body in the trunk." But no, I had to stay half an hour to suffer a conversation that was worse than having your bunions hammered with a burning hot pile driver.

Even better, as I whispered goodbye to Virginia, "Have fun, I'll be back to pick you up at seven," the birthday girl's father came in loaded with trays, and cast me a look worse than a stray dog with mange in a spring thunderstorm.

"Where the hell are you going?" the look said. "You can't leave me alone with them. There's a blood pact between all men in the world, and you know it, you bastard. Stay here, and we'll share our unfortunate lot like real brothers."

I looked back at him, and my look said, "Like hell, this is your party and your daughter, and I had one of these things not so long ago and I don't recall seeing you in my house, jerk. And be grateful I don't trip you and make you drop all those mini sandwiches with mini toothpick flags stuck in them."

And his eyes shot back, "That's not cool, why do you have to be so stubborn? Everyone makes mistakes, and I didn't even know about your party—my wife only tells me what she wants and she kept the invitation from me, I'm sorry."

So I gave in to sentiment and went over and took half the trays, and when we set them on the big table, he smiled at me conspiratorially, elbowing me and saying, "Should we have a beer? Huh, huh?"

And already at "be—" you could feel the blast of wind from twenty-four mothers turning toward him in unison and giving him the stink eye as if he had cursed in church, or rather, at Sunday school.

"Beer at a kids' party, did you say? Shame on you!" said their forty-eight accusatory eyes. At which I caught the ball mid-bounce, put a hand on his arm, brother-like, and told him, "Hey, thanks, but I've got minestrone on the stove at home and I've still got to stop at the store."

At that moment, the twenty-four looks instantly transformed into expressions of exuberant sympathy and I came out strutting like a rooster, stroked by twenty-four pairs of eyelashes of mothers who had just heard the word "minestrone" from an Italian man without it being in the sentence: "Hey, is the minestrone ready yet?"

I said goodbye to Virginia again with a kiss on the forehead and went out into the crisp evening air. As I was heading to the car, some kid threw a noisemaker at me, making me jump, and I nearly fell over. I couldn't help but think that bastard had sent a hit man after me as a warning. "Come back inside," that noisemaker said, "or things will go south fast—remember we have your daughter!"

But I didn't let myself be intimidated. Decisive, I got in the car, drove off, and went to the discount store, where I did the grocery shopping, like a real man. Then I went home, washed the dishes, answered three e-mails, fed the dogs, and it was already time to go pick her up.

"Did you have fun, Virginia?" I asked, helping her into her coat.

"Yes, Papa. Will you make me pizza tonight?"

"There's not enough time for the dough to rise tonight, but I'll make it for you tomorrow, I promise."

She smiled and we said goodbye to everyone and rushed up the stairs as Maria Carla looked at us as if to say, "Please take me with you, even if it's in the trunk next to the body!" And the birthday girl's mother was yelling at her husband, who had just eaten the last mortadella sandwich without asking.

Garrett
(Or, on Common Sense)

have two dogs. A few years ago I had four, but then, life happened.

The bigger of the two is called Garrett in homage to a friend of ours who, at the time, was at the Lucca Comics convention presenting a comic miniseries with that title.

Garrett is actually Tuscan, because we adopted him at the Lucca convention that year.

Paola was pregnant with Virginia, and she'd said she wanted to have lunch away from the comics crowd that day. We braved the outskirts of town, discovering that there was also intelligent life outside. We found a nice little place called ScusaAmeri—it's still there, I checked—where Paola ordered a big plate of sausages and frankfurters with chips, since salad was off limits during pregnancy. Whereas I wasn't pregnant, but you know, solidarity.

Behind me there was a bulletin board with announcements. Among the "1986 Tuareg dirt bike for sale, like new" and "does God exist or is he just pretending" announcements, a photo of a sweet fuzzy face stood out. It looked like a cross between a mushroom and Fozzie Bear from the Muppets. Paola took the flyer and started staring at it with sentimental, glistening eyes. The sheet with the photo of the little face read: "Three-month-old lost puppy in need of a forever home. If I don't find anyone I'll have to take him to the shelter, because I can't keep him." There was a phone number, followed by "ask for Eleonora."

It should be mentioned that we already had three dogs at the time. For that very reason, we had just gone and rented a run-down old house because it had a giant yard.

Paola looked at me imploringly. I'd read somewhere that it's better not to say no to pregnant women. I thought of the 1600-square-foot yard, the old pines. Of my parents, who would say indignantly, "What? You have three already!" Of the number of turds that were enough as it was and that I would have to pick up off the lawn every day. Of the coming daughter who would turn our lives upside down in a way that wasn't possible to imagine yet, not even a little. Despite that, in a surge of love and tenderness I thought, "Why not, what's a little more poop?"

"Okay, call," I said.

"Are you serious?" Paola said.

"No, no, call, really," I said. "Let's at least see him, why not."

Paola threw her arms around my neck and then called—maybe not in that order.

The girl arrived in her Ford Fiesta fifteen minutes later. The puppy from the photo leapt out of the back. Funny, sweet, and adorable. The only odd detail was his enormous paws, totally disproportionate compared with the rest of his body. I looked at Paola, perplexed.

"You said he should stay more or less this same size, right?" I asked.

"Um, yeah. Yeah. It's a breed that stays pretty small . . ." Paola said.

"Okay," I said.

We thanked the girl and left with a hug and an exchange of numbers and addresses. Suddenly we had a dog, in Lucca.

On the way back, Garrett was very good. He didn't make a peep, didn't bark once, didn't pee in the car. He stayed curled up in the backseat, with a placid expression just like Fozzie from the Muppets.

Once he got home, after meeting his suspicious furry companions, he peed on the rug in welcome.

"He's a puppy," Paola said. "He's still learning."

"Okay," I said.

The next day he took a shit in the office.

Aside from these early accidents, Garrett settled in quickly. Lana ignored him, Skippy also did, for the most part—he only acted out when Garrett sat on his head—whereas Lippa, our medium-sized dog, decided he was her playmate. Within two weeks, Garrett was as big as she was. After three months, he was a seventy-five-pound dog with a nocturnal passion for cats and pinecones and was notorious throughout the neighborhood.

He was constantly digging in the perennially tall grass in the yard, his ears in the wind, chasing anything that moved: blackbirds, bees, butterflies. The postman.

His favorite, can't-miss time was around four in the afternoon, a few times a week.

Garrett set up camp in the corner where the fence ended, as if waiting for something to appear. After a while a little girl on her bike would show up. She must have been nine or ten, I never asked. Garrett would jump on the wall with his big paws and lean his whole upper body out as far as he could. The girl would throw her bike on the ground, climb up the wall, and hug him for several minutes.

I would look on from the office window, and in those moments I felt a strong awareness that, even if I died tomorrow, no one could deprive me of the fact that I'd saved at least one life in my life. Just by deliberately going against that thing that too many call "common sense."

Using this tried and true technique, I quit my job one snowy day to devote myself to comics, the year after that we adopted Cordelia (after the anime *Anne of Green Gables*—if you've seen it, you'll know what I mean—) then I agreed to have another child and then another since sleep, really, is overrated.

Karma

When I was working in public administration, I was able to plan several piazzas.

The significance of planning a piazza may be beyond some people. For them, just know that the empty spaces must be carefully thought out. Urban empty spaces are much more important than the crowded ones, because they're what gives life to the architectural fabric of an area—in Italy it would make more sense to say structural fabric, but let's not split hairs.

The planning started with initial brainstorming— "we have to make a piazza"—periodically interspersed with what the administrators (the equivalent of a city mayor, let's say) loved to call by the English word "checks," because they'd heard it on TV.

An example of a check:

"Everything okay?" they'd ask, peeking into my office.

"Everything's okay," I always replied.

When the project was finished, I had to face a whole series of inevitable, finicky objections, like:

"No, we can't have a fountain there, the filter would get clogged with oleander leaves."

"Then just cut the leaves every couple of weeks."

"No, no, it's better not to have one at all. Come to think of it, let's scrap the oleander too."

Stuff like that.

After these obstacles, I invariably had to deal with the planning commission jumping down my throat.

The problem wasn't so much the initial meeting with the various administrators as much as the public assembly where residents had the opportunity to express their views on major projects.

In those cases, the greatest difficulty was always adapting the technical language and rationale for the audience. This was very important, because if I wasn't able to make myself understood, there was no hope.

I remember one time I managed to win over a guy who was pissed off because according to him, too much funding was being allocated to culture.

"People can read books in their own homes!"

I managed to change his mind by explaining to him simply that the money wouldn't be used *only* for books, but that, for example, the salami festival was also culture. I got lucky and my example was right on target, because he was especially a fan of risotto with salami and played in the darts tournament at the festival every year.

Back to the piazzas. I recall one winter evening in

particular when a guy in the public commission so politely explained to me during an assembly that "planning is bullshit! Things get done faster if you just do them! What does it take to put in a couple trees and a few benches?"

Now, to me, one of the three things in the world that *really* irritate the hell out of me is when, even indirectly, my profession or its utility is called into question. My profession, at the time, was urban planning.

I took the mic.

"What do you do?" I said.

"I own a bar," he said.

"Great. How do you make a negroni?"

"What does that have to do with anything?"

"It's just a question. How do you make a negroni? Do you know or not?" I insisted.

"Ehhh, boy!" he said. "I practically invented the negroni. It's a third gin, a third Campari, and a third red vermouth."

"Perfect. And the orange slice?"

"Yeah, that too, at the end. Goes without saying."

"Wonderful. Thank you for just having illustrated to us the plan for a negroni."

"Huh?"

The room laughed. The piazza was approved by an overwhelming majority.

I saw the bar guy in my office six months later when he came to protest the roundabout that had been created in front of his shop while he was on vacation. Without wasting any time to make a real plan, simply putting it on the books as ordinary maintenance.

The traffic circle was not too big, very green, and directly across from this guy's bar.

The bar was called L'angolo—The Corner.

Still today, thinking about it makes me laugh uncontrollably.

A!

Melania is almost two but the only word she says is: "A!"

The oldest of the three, by contrast, debuted at one with: "What's in a name? That which we call a rose, By any other name would smell as sweet."

The second, at thirteen months, quoted straight from Dante.

Melania, on the other hand, couldn't care less. She's also amazing for that reason, because she doesn't even seem interested in speaking. Anyway, why should she, when she can command the entire universe with a single vowel? In fact, what's incredible is that she makes herself understood anyway, perfectly, just by modifying the tone of her voice.

For example:

"A!" (Hi!)

"aA!" (Pick me up, now!)

"AaA!" (Pick me up, I said, you vicious imbecile!)

"AaaaaaaaaAAAA!" (I love it!)

"AAAAAAAAAAAAAAAAAAAAAAAAAAAAA!!"
(Gross!)

"AaaaaaAA. A!" (I'm hungry!)

And so on.

The only exception to Vowel-land is water. Because Melania, to ask for water, snorts. She makes this hilarious sound with her nose and her eyes squint and she breathes in and out very quickly, like a bloodhound sniffing.

So that means: I'm thirsty.

The funny thing is that at her nursery school, where she goes every day, there are also older kids who speak pretty well. The hope was that Melania would be influenced by them and her language would evolve (not her powers of expression, I mean actual words). The result? All the kids at the school, even the ones who could talk perfectly well, snort when they want water.

Paola and I would never admit that it doesn't really bother us at all. Because this "delay" cradles us in the illusion of still having a little baby and helps us feel young. And besides that, Melania runs like a fireball, eats like a dragon, climbs up on the shelves, manages to reach inaccessible objects, knows how to call her grandparents and my publisher, and last week she wrote all over the couch with a red felt-tip pen filched from her mother. The truth is that our daughter is Stewie from *Family Guy* in disguise.

The Camera

We gave Virginia a used digital camera.

I gave it to her barely half an hour ago. Since then, she has taken about thirty pictures of me and about twenty of Melania. After the fifth I'd already gone blind. Around the fifteenth she discovered how to turn off the flash. Now she's figured out how to take videos and she's recording me as I write on the iPad. The video is a sort of interview.

"Tell us, Mr. Bussola, do you like living in this house?"

"Yes."

"And are you happy to have three daughters?"

"Very happy."

"And are you happy to have the mom we have?"

"Definitely."

"Good, good. Listen, now the most important question."

"Yes?"

"Can we get pizza tonight?"

Heartbeats

It happens almost every morning. I go into her room to wake her up, wait for a moment listening in the dark, and if I don't hear anything, not even breathing, and she's not moving, I put my hand on her back, palm flat, and she doesn't move, so I press softly, jiggle her a tiny bit, and after about a second she snaps to life in her crib like a spring. In that endless second, my heart skips a beat. It was the same with the other two—it's something that lasts until they're about three years old. If I add up all the lost heartbeats, it comes out to a week of life. A dad thing.

Come By

My phone rings, there's no number.

"Hello?"

"Hello, good morning. Mr. Matteo Bussola?"

"Speaking, who's this?"

"Oh, hi. This is Giacomo from UniCredit."

"Good morning, Giacomo."

"Good morning. I'm calling to ask if you might be able to come by the office next week, the Via dell'Artigliere branch."

"Oh, Jesus. What for? Have you found me out?"

"Found you out?"

"Forget it, it was a joke."

"Oh."

"No, I mean, why do I need to come by?"

"Because if you do, we'll be happy to show you all our wonderful new products, which I'm sure you'll be interested in hearing about."

"Products?"

"That's right. Our new bonds, new line of credit cards, new reduced interest rate loans, and so on."

"Oh, no, then I won't stop by."

"Sorry?"

"No, it's just that, see, I'm poor. You won't be giving me any credit cards and you definitely won't be approving me for any loans."

"What do you mean, Mr. Bussola? If you've been a longtime customer with us, I can guarantee you that generally speaking, and especially with these new offers, it should be no problem."

"Look, Giacomo. You already barely gave me a loan once, eight years ago. And you only approved my application because I worked in public administration."

"Oh, are you a government employee? Then I can personally guarantee that you'll have no problem securing a loan."

"Worked."

"What?"

"Worked in public administration."

"Oh, I'm sorry. Damn budget cuts . . ."

"No, that's not it. I quit."

"You . . . quit? A permanent position?!"

"Yeah."

"My Lord. And, if I may, what do you do now?"

"I draw comics."

"What?

"Draw. Comics."

"You draw?"

"Yes. Comics."

"Whoa, really? That's great. You know, I have the entire Mickey Mouse collection. Well, almost. And I have a few books of . . . um, what's it called? My brother bought them. Mark Mister."

"*Martin Mystère*."

"That's it. But go on. What comic do you draw?"

"I work for that same publisher, Sergio Bonelli Editore, and also for a French publisher."

"French?"

"Yes. I realize it may be hard to believe, but they read comics over there too."

"Well, what do you know, that's so cool. And what do you draw for Binello Editrice?"

"I draw a comic set in Africa that's called *Adam Wild*."

"Oh, I don't know that one."

"I didn't think so. What about *Dylan Dog*?"

"Yeah, yeah, I know that one! The one with the monsters. You draw that too?"

"No. My partner writes it."

"No way!"

"I swear."

"So what do you mean she writes it?"

"She writes the stories."

"The stories?"

"She scripts them. She comes up with the plot and the dialogue and then she writes a detailed script that gets sent to an illustrator who draws it."

"Oh. So she writes the words in the bubbles, basically."

"No, that's done by the . . . Actually, yes. Yes, she puts the words in the bubbles, yeah. Every day. A real pain, you can imagine."

"I'm sure. Well, wow. What a couple!"

"Yep."

"All right. Listen. As I was saying, I think you'll have no problem."

"Trust me, you won't give me a loan."

"That's not true, Mr. Bussola! Why so negative? The conditions have changed completely, you know. All we need is a pay stub."

"I don't have one."

"What?"

"I don't have a pay stub. Comics artists work freelance. I'm not an employee, I get paid, minus withholding tax, on delivery."

"Oh. That's okay, if you can show us your average earnings over a certain period, two years, let's say, and it's consistent, I'm sure there's no problem. And then maybe your estimated pension."

"I don't have one."

"What?"

"Comics artists don't have a pension."

"You mean, you don't get retirement?"

"No. We don't get paid vacation either."

"What if you get sick?"

"I stick it out."

"Severance?"

"A handshake, if things end well."

"A handshake? All right, listen. Just come by, I'm sure we can find the right solution. In fact, if you give me your account number, I'll check right away and you'll be sure to be approved."

"The number is xxxxxxxxxxxx."

"Okay, there we go."

"You see my account history?"

"Oh."

"What do you say, then? Should I come by?"

"Mr. Bussola?"

"Yes?"

"Did you make a withdrawal of twenty euros this morning?"

"Yes."

"You made a cash withdrawal of twenty euros?"

"Why, is that not allowed? I had to get the latest *Ken Parker* and some olive oil."

"Are you aware that your current account balance is two euros and fifty cents?"

"Really? I thought it was less. I'll come by tomorrow then, yeah? What time would work?"

"Have a nice day."

"Hello?"

And they say I'm negative.

The Man in the Car

slept one hour last night.

Melania had a high fever and slept in bed with us, first huddled up against her mom, kicking at me, then draped over my chest and coughing in my face. Around two in the morning I threw in the towel, built a wall of pillows around her for her to kick, and got up. I went to the kitchen to make myself a coffee, but a weak one; I didn't want to give up all hope for sleep. I went to the office for a while and started penciling a new page. I didn't notice the time go by and suddenly it was eight. I went upstairs, made another coffee, and went to check on things in the bedroom. Paola and Melania were still sleeping, immersed in the unnatural silence of the house due to the absence of the older girls, who were in the mountains with their grandparents for the weekend. Looking in at them from the doorway, I saw them illuminated in the dark from the hallway light, and they looked like they were fused, just one body, as if they were joined again. At some point Paola realized I was there and asked me to heat up some milk. When I went back, Melania was awake, Paola gave her the bottle, and I remembered I needed to go out to buy envelopes.

In the car, going down the hill, I noticed the bright blue sky and a brilliant light, which seemed intensified by the winter air. Once I got to the tree-lined boulevard, I saw a green Fiat Punto stopped in the middle of the road. My first thought was an accident, or breakdown, or overly adventurous parking attempt. But when I came up alongside the car, sitting in the driver's seat was an elderly man with a brown cap. Completely still, with the car off and his chin resting on the steering wheel. "Maybe there's something wrong," I thought. It occurred to me that maybe he was sick. I was about to get out and check, when I noticed that the man was looking at something. His face was lit up, he was looking toward the sky with his eyes half closed and crying and smiling at the same time.

He was staring at the sun, or at least so it seemed, sitting in his car right where you could see the sun rising above the hill, moving along the road like the spotlight at a concert.

"I wonder what he's thinking," I said to myself. The look on his face was beautiful. Then a car honked and sped around. Then another. A line of cars had formed behind us, which I hadn't noticed because of the hazy traces of sleep.

I shifted into first and sped off, but the man stayed put.

When I left the stationery store, I decided that since I was already out, I might as well stop at the grocery store. I got some milk, celery to make broth, and some oranges on sale.

On the way home, I stopped under the trees on the boulevard to eat an orange in the car.

The man wasn't there anymore. Now it was me.

Four

Ginevra turns four today.

I just dropped her off at nursery school, but for her special day, we're going to pick her up early. That way she can have a little lunchtime celebration with her grandparents, and then after four, a real party at home with her friends.

When we were by the cubbies, she asked, "Daddy, am I grown up now that I'm four?"

I didn't know how to respond, because I wasn't sure what she wanted to hear. I ventured, "Yes," but she went on immediately, saying: "I don't want to grow up, I want to stay little."

At which I, after every reassurance about how great growing up is, decided to forget the didactic clichés and fatherly inanities like: "That's just the way it is." I sat down on the bench, put her on my knee, and as if I were about to tell her a secret, said: "You know what, Ginevra? No matter how big a person gets, if she wants to, she can stay little anyway. Even as an adult."

"How?"

"You just have to keep doing the things you like best."

She looked me right in the eye and didn't say anything, but I knew she had understood. I took her to class, and when I was about to leave, she turned to me and said, "Daddy, when I get home today, can I paint cherries?"

And I told her, "Sure you can, Ginevra."

Then I went out, went around the building, and stood in front of the window for our goodbye leap. She laughed at me through the glass and I just thought, "Please, stay like this forever," because what I like most in the world is taking her to nursery school and seeing her through that window jump up and smile with those tiny teeth, as if that sight were really the only thing that could save me from becoming a sad, hopeless grown-up.

The Case

Virginia made a case for her camera.

She took a cardboard box, like a shoebox but narrower, filled it with balled-up paper, then placed the camera inside and put the lid on top. Then she wrapped it with some colored paper, taping the edges just like a Christmas present. When she came and showed it to me, all proud, I pointed out that perhaps it wasn't very practical as a case, since she would have to take off the tape and the wrap, open the lid, and dig through the balled-up paper every time she wanted to use the camera. Virginia looked at me as if I were an idiot and said: "So what? It'll take longer to open, but at least it's pretty!"

In the moment, I admit, I wanted to laugh. Then I thought about it a little more and came to the conclusion, as in now I've seen the light, that without realizing it my daughter had reminded me of an essential lesson: Beauty is never easy. And if you don't choose it just because it might take longer to open, or to achieve, all the time you save avoiding it will never be a triumph, but the most clamorous of defeats.

Why Does Mom . . . ?

"Papa, why does Mom always go to Milan for work?"

"She doesn't always go, Ginevra. She goes like once a month."

"And why are you always here?"

"Well, because I work from home and send my drawings to my editor; I don't need to go all the way to Milan for work stuff. And then that way I can stay with you, right?"

She looks at me pointedly.

"They don't want to talk to you, do they, Daddy?"

"Nope."

"Can we get pizza tonight?"

"All right, Ginevra. I'll call in a little bit."

"I hope they answer you."

The Crooked Tree

In our garden, there's a crooked tree.

The tree is very tall and leaning dangerously toward the house. When there's a strong wind, it sways ominously.

I called a specialized company this summer. The original idea was to get to the root of the problem by cutting down the tree. But Paola wasn't happy. She kept grumbling that, well, killing a fir tree, a living healthy plant, just to reduce a risk that may never present itself just wasn't right. So I got two estimates: one to cut it down, and another to prune it. It so happened that pruning it cost less and we decided to take it as a sign.

They came on a sunny day in July. They climbed up, trimmed the tree more or less completely of all its excess foliage and overly heavy or prominent branches. They reduced the wind effect. They rebalanced it, giving us specific guarantees as to its stability and promising us that nothing would happen.

"Even if, of course, there are no guarantees when it comes to nature."

In reality, from July to December the tree just got more and more crooked. Now that it's almost all trunk, it's even more obvious. If you look at the tree from ten yards away, you see that it's leaning over and curved like a bow. When the wind picks up, it sways even more ominously than before.

Yesterday afternoon, before going to pick up the girls, I called Paola into the yard. "Come look at this," I said. I took her to the spot with the clearest view and pointed to the tree, my finger tracing the curve of the trunk in the air.

"Come on, let it go! That's just how the tree is, okay?" she said. "Has anyone ever made you feel bad about being crooked? And we keep you around anyway."

I looked at her, smiling. Not so much because I completely agreed, but because in life, the moments when you really remember the reasons why you're with someone, the times when you really feel it, are four or five max, if you're lucky.

When Paola and I first met, we were two crooked trees. We decided to get together, but it immediately became clear that neither would be able to straighten out the other, that our two crooked trees together wouldn't make one straight one.

But, with each supporting the other, we made a tree

house. The tree house lives on and gets bigger every day. Sometimes it sways when the wind gets strong.

So far, no one has been able to fell it.

Beer

Paola is going to the store. I ask her to get me some beer.

Last time, I told her to "get the kind in the yellow cans" because Paola doesn't drink and doesn't know brands, and she came back with a silver can that makes Peroni seem like a craft Weiss made with malted barley handpicked by flaxen-haired maidens on dewy nights under the full moon. So this time I give her more specific instructions.

I tell her, "Get *any* beer *except* the one in the silver can, please. In particular, if you want to be safe, get the one in the blue and gray can. Or the yellow one."

Tonight I open the fridge and get a beer. The can is black as death with a blue stripe in the middle. On the front there's a giant 12, which she must have mistaken for the jersey number of a soccer player from Inter. However, it indicates that the beer in question is a twelve-proof triple malt. Basically, a can of wine. I'd had this kind three or four times before, and that was during the period when I kept randomly writing cheesy status updates on Facebook between seven and eight in the evening. Then I think I got hepatitis.

I dig through the fridge hopelessly, looking for I don't know what exactly. At some point, pushing aside the anchovies and the pickles, my hand meets another can. I take a closer look. It's almost all red but it's not Coke. Thank the Lord, maybe in a rush of exuberance and affection Paola bought me a second beer!

I read the brand. Never heard of it. I look at the alcohol percentage to avoid any surprises.

It's nonalcoholic.

Sentimental Alphabet

My life is always organized according to the same schedule.

The schedule revolves mostly around the girls.

The morning is devoted to getting them ready for school and carting them around. Virginia has volleyball on Thursdays, trips to her grandparents on Saturdays, and every afternoon, homework and a snack. Every night, games in Mom and Dad's bed, and stories and songs. At lunch and dinner, striving step-by-step to introduce new foods, battling on the slippery ground that is taste.

On Tuesday afternoons, Paola takes Virginia and Ginevra to the pool. I stay at home with Melania.

When we're by ourselves, Melania takes over. She's like a beaver used to swimming between log dams that suddenly gets thrown into the open sea. First she wants to draw, then she wants to run, then she asks for cookies, then she's thirsty, then she wants to write on the television, then she wants to be held but she also wants to be put down. She wants everything and nothing, she's energy in its pure state, elemental joy, perpetual motion powered by a dynamo of crumbs.

I adore her beyond all measure and limit. Because I have the total—on some days almost painful—awareness that she will be our last little girl. After this, it's just the flatlands of adolescence: slammed doors, stupid dolls, and friendship bracelets. I like Simone, no I mean Mattia; shut up, Dad; I don't want any salad; and the rest of the repertoire.

Whereas now I can still enjoy Melania completely and she can enjoy me completely. She knows I'm the weak link—she had that figured out the first time I picked her up in the hospital and changed her with one hand while she peed on the other, before the amused eyes of the obstetrician.

Things change, children grow up, just like how all good things must come to an end, two heads are better than one, and there's no time like the present. And right now it's Tuesday afternoon.

So tonight I'll work, but right now I'll enjoy the moments that will stave off future regrets. I say my sentimental alphabet as I build towers of Legos.

All the letters in sentimental alphabets end with an exclamation point.

The first letter is *A!* and it makes a round sound.

Feet and Music

"Daddy, why is Saint Lucia blind?"

"Eh, Ginevra, because a bad person hurt her eyes to make her do something she didn't want to do."

"And did she do it?"

"No."

"But if she's blind, how can she read the notes on the presents kids give her?"

"Oh, well, I think her assistant reads them to her, the coachman who leads her mule."

"And what's his name?"

"The assistant? Castaldo."

"Does she love him?"

"Who?"

"Saint Lucia, does she love him?"

"Oh, geez, Ginevra, I don't know. . . . I've never thought about it. I'm sure she's fond of him, of course, but I don't know if they're a couple or anything."

"But if she's blind, how can she love him?"

"Huh? What do you mean?"

"If she can't see him. Maybe he's ugly."

"Listen, peanut. Do you love Daddy?"

"No."

"Okay. Different question. Do you love Mommy?"

"Yes."

"When you close your eyes, do you still love her?"

"Yes."

"Okay, well it's the same thing with grown-up love, Ginevra. It's not just about what you see, but how you feel even with things you can't see, like when you listen to your songs with your earphones."

I observe her as she contemplates my words.

"So love is like music, Daddy?"

"Sort of, yes. But you can't feel it through your ears."

"Well, how then?"

"Well, through everything. Even your nose. Your hands. Your feet."

"No way! How can you feel it with your feet?"

"I'll give you an example. You know what girlfriends do to their boyfriends, to test whether they really love them? Your mom always did it to me."

"What?"

"At the beginning, when I used to go to her house, or she would come to mine, and she slept over, your mom would always put her freezing feet on my back or my legs."

"And what did you do?"

"I left them there and warmed them."

"But didn't they make you really cold?"

"A little, sure."

"So when Mommy put her feet on you, you heard music, Daddy?"

"Always."

On Comics and
Fathers and Sons

"What do you mean, comics?" the father says.

"Comics," says the son.

"Like the comics in the papers?" the father says.

"Yeah, like those," the son says.

"Okay, but what do you mean you want to *make* them?" the father says.

"I want to make them. Draw them. Invent them. I want to make my living by coming up with stories and putting them on paper. And I'd like to draw Tex one day too," the son says.

"Tex?" the father says.

"Tex, the cowboy. The one with the . . ."

"I *know* who Tex is," the father says.

"Well then," the son says.

"Well then, did you know," the father says, "that comics artists have terrible lives?"

"That's not true," the son says.

"Yes it is!" the father says. "Professional cartoonists spend their whole lives sitting hunched over a desk. They never go out, they even draw at night, they become antisocial. Nerds. They end up convinced that that's their whole world, all in their pages, and that's it."

"You mean like you and the poems you write in your notebooks?" the son says.

"What does poetry have to do with it?" the father says. "Poetry is poetry. I hope you don't mean to compare cartoons to poetry, for God's sake! I need those poems. They've been my way of enduring this disgusting world and a job I didn't choose these past forty years," the father says.

"Exactly," the son says.

"Exactly what?" the father says.

"I'm choosing. That's what I'm telling you now, you get it?"

"What?"

"My job! I'm choosing it. I'm telling you. And I'm also choosing my way of enduring. I'll do both things at the same time. My work will be my way of enduring!" the son shouts.

"But do you realize that comics artists are poor? Huh? Do you realize that, at least? Do you realize they don't get retirement? And when you have kids? Huh? How will you get by then?" the father insists.

"That's not true," the son says. "There are comics artists who've become millionaires! Not that many, but they exist. And anyway, Dad, are you so rich?"

"What does that matter?" the father says.

"And you had kids, right?" the son says.

". . ." the father says nothing.

"See?" the son says.

"All right, I get it! Make your comics then! But at least get a degree first!"

"What do I need it for, though?"

"To make better comics," the father says. "And to have something to rebel against. If you don't, you'd risk making crappy comics."

The son looks at the father, incredulous. The father looks at the TV, incredulous. They've been interviewing some disgusting politician on the news for five minutes. He has an urge to write a poem.

"Anyway," the father says, "don't you become one of those millionaires. Do me a favor. Make comics, if you really have to. But just aim for a normal life."

"Huh? Why?" the son says.

"Because millionaires are all assholes," the father says. "And I'll already have a comics nerd son. But at least he won't be an asshole, not that."

The son bursts out laughing. After a minute, the father laughs too.

For a moment it's as if they're the same age.

"Coffee" Coffee

changed to a new coffee brand.

I buy it at the discount market. It's called "Coffee" coffee.

"Coffee" coffee comes in an ochre yellow package and it's next to the cleaners. But it's never on sale; you always pay full price: ninety cents. With better-known coffee brands, when you read the ingredients on the back of the package, they usually say: 70 percent robusta, 30 percent arabica. Or vice versa. Roasting level, bean origin, an awkward attempt to describe aroma and characteristics.

On the "Coffee" coffee package, it says, INGREDIENTS: COFFEE.

But let me tell you, although the name proudly asserts the opposite, I'm not so sure it's really coffee coffee. In fact, when I open the bag, instead of being hit by an aromatic gust of roast and caffeine that fills my nose for a full thirty seconds and invariably takes me back to my nonna's tiramisu, "Coffee" coffee just emanates a faint singed smell, like burned toast.

When I put it in the pot I've been using for seventeen years, "Coffee" coffee displays two distinct colors, like the stripes in Colgate. There's a darker brown line and a visibly lighter one. They don't mix, their nonfluid state condemns them to this sedimentary separation.

They coexist.

The theory I've developed is that the lighter one is actually coffee coffee, whereas I have two hypotheses for the darker one: the first is that the manufacturer roasts not only the beans—the lighter part—but also other parts of the plant, like the pods, the leaves, or the stems (at the moment I don't know exactly what a coffee plant is like, sorry). The second hypothesis is the same one you're thinking.

"Coffee" coffee, when it rises in the pot, doesn't make that proverbial hiss that consecrates waking up in the morning. It just rises. That depresses me a little. But at five-thirty in the morning it has the advantage that I can make my coffee in total silence.

"Coffee" coffee, when you drink it, tastes like coffee. But it's a mystery. If you smell it from your steaming cup, it's like sniffing a tire that's been lit on fire with grappa. Yet the taste is unmistakably coffee.

Having tried this, I decided that next week I want to try "Chips" chips. Even if they smell like fried bananas when you open the bag, they shouldn't be too bad.

Suddenly I imagine a world of redundancies where everything is called by its name twice. Where there are coffee coffees, house houses, shit shits. A world that doesn't care about synthesis, where it would take twice as long to speak, where Facebook debates would be interminable, and where watching an entire episode of *Crossfire* would drive you to suicide.

But also a world where *Good Will Hunting* would last four hours and Murakami's *Norwegian Wood* would give me shelter for my whole summer at twenty-two, like a shadow. Where songs would be very long and slow dances would go on forever.

An imaginary world where we could look deep into the eye eyes of that one woman and tell her, without being afraid of feeling ridiculous:

"I love love you."

No comparison.

Braids

I n the car, on the way to nursery school:

"Daddy, why did Mommy get up this morning even though she has a fever?"

"Well, Ginevra, she got up just to do your braids, imagine that."

"Why didn't you do them for me?"

"Because unfortunately, dads aren't very good at braiding hair."

"Daddy! What do you mean?"

"It's true, Ginevra. Generally, dads are a disaster with hair. I am, for sure."

We go in, sit down on the bench, and I put on her little smock.

Across from us there's a father fumbling with his daughter. He just took off her hat, evidently in a hurry—amateur—demolishing the fine handiwork of his wife, or grandmother, or older sister, I don't know. Clearly not his. His desperation is painted on his face.

"Jesus, Emma. Over here! Come here so I can fix you, Jesus!"

He's trying to fix two little ponytails with some ninja technique I can't figure out. It's incredible, it's almost like he can't wrap the elastic around twice, one of the three basic techniques of the samurai hairdressing school. He's sweating.

At some point he turns to me with a pleading look on his face, whether intentional or not I'm not sure. Maybe he's just staring into space trying to remember the second law of thermodynamics.

"Need a hand?" I ask instinctively.

"Oh! Yeah, sure, thank you! I'm not so . . ."

"Don't worry, me neither."

We smile in complicity, to relieve our sense of inadequacy.

We work together for a few minutes, him on the left ponytail and me on the right. Emma enters the classroom as if she's just come out of the dryer, but he appears satisfied.

When the other dad leaves, I take my daughter aside.

"See that, Ginevra?"

This is on purpose, glancing over at the girl as if to say, "I told you, dads . . ."

My daughter studies the girl's hair, with a gleam in her eyes and a dreamy expression.

"Yeah! That girl's hair looks so pretty!"

Okay, it's decided: I'm on braid duty starting tomorrow. Or it's back to the old pirate bandanna.

Maybe I'll bring a few extra. I bet I'd make a killing at the cubbies.

What Women Don't Say

Last night I fell victim to the worst stomachache I can remember.

It came on suddenly after dinner, numbing my body, gradually taking my breath away, like being punched over and over. All I wanted to do was lie still under the covers with my hands on my stomach. But that night Melania, who usually sleeps soundly without any problem, kept waking up. She would wake up and start to cry. We brought her to bed with us, but she kept on. She didn't want milk or cookies or cartoons, nothing. She nodded off five times and we put her back in her crib, but started crying again after a couple minutes. So I said to Paola, who hadn't felt well herself that day, that since my stomachache was keeping me up anyway, it didn't make sense for us both to stay awake with the baby—at least she should get some sleep. I picked up the crying Melania and she held her arms out to me like she always does, in that way that fills a father's heart with paternal pride. Saving some damsel from a tower could never compare to the feeling of saving one's daughter from the darkness of her crib. We went into the living room and I tried putting on some cartoons and rocking her a little, but it was no use. Then I lay down on my back and put her on my chest. I pulled the two blankets on the sofa over us and we curled up like cats. Melania closed her eyes. After a while, the warmth of her body began to dull my pain, as if she were a little hot water bottle. Her breath on my face, her head nestled in the crook of my neck, our diaphragms moving in unison, the uncomfortable yet perfectly natural position of our bodies transported me into a calm, dense dimension. These are the sort of in-between moments that fathers know well. The privileges of men who embrace their maternal side. Holding back a sob in your chest, feeling it melt away and be overtaken by a restless and then a deep sleep. Giving in to the precipice of the present and being there, body to body at three in the morning, cartoon jingles in the background, the living room lamp in your eyes, the awkward pillow you want to adjust but can't. Quickly realizing that a chance position can become the perfect one, the best observation point for everything else.

What mothers don't imagine is that when fathers get up at three in the morning to comfort their children, it's not to be considerate or let them sleep. It's to get back that feeling. Breathing, snuggling, enjoying the moment. To feel a little closer to something that deep down they never had and never will.

Because what women don't say is nothing compared to what men don't know.

Eyes Like Andy Garcia

I go pick up Virginia from school because she has volleyball on Thursdays.

While I'm out front waiting for the bell to ring, I notice a mom glancing over at me every now and then. She's glancing around looking lost. Then she turns back in my direction and eventually comes over. She's blond, wearing a gray jacket with dark-bordered pockets and a soft white hat. She looks about forty. Once she's up close I see some faint freckles. She has blue-rimmed glasses that make her eyes appear bigger. I look like Santa Claus in regular clothes, waiting to hear back about his prostate exam.

"Hi," she says. "Do you happen to know if they're getting out late today?"

"No," I say. "I don't think so."

"Because they're usually out by now, right?"

"I don't know," I say. "I don't wear a watch. I just go wait by the plane tree."

"Oh. How . . . Zen."

"No, no, not Zen. I just hate watches, that's all."

"Oh. Well, you must have a cell phone to check the time, right?"

"I do," I say. "It's on my desk at home."

"Ha ha." When she laughs I notice a slight gap between her incisors.

"Anyway all the parents are here and they don't seem worried," I say. "So I'm sure everything's fine."

"It is strange, though. They should have gotten out by now."

"Look, maybe you should ask someone else. I only come on Thursdays, and honestly I don't know if there's been a change in the schedule."

"Okay."

She doesn't move. She folds her arms over her chest and waits beside me under the tree. Five minutes go by and nothing happens.

"Anyway, I'm Francesca," she says, offering her hand.

"Matteo," I say.

"What class is your son in?"

"Daughter."

"Oh, you have a daughter too?"

"I have three."

"Wow!"

"Yep."

"Sorry, can I tell you something without you taking it the wrong way?"

"Shoot."

"You have eyes just like Andy Garcia."

"Oh," I say. "Thanks?"

"Yeah, I meant it as a compliment," she says. "Definitely."

The bell rings. The teachers lead the children single file into the yard. Virginia sees me, asks permission to leave, then comes running over.

"Hi, Daddy!" she says to me.

"Hi, sweetheart. We have to hurry; otherwise you'll be late for volleyball."

"Okay!" she says.

I turn for a second to say goodbye to the mom, but she's no longer there. I catch sight of her near the gate across the yard. She's holding a little girl by the hand, a fifth grader or so, in any case certainly older than mine. Before leaving, she turns in our direction. She waves goodbye. I do the same.

"Daddy," Virginia says.

"Yes?"

"You have a giant booger hanging out of your nose."

"Really?"

I wipe my nose with my hand and then with a tissue. I go over the entire conversation I just had, picturing myself with a giant booger hanging out of my nose.

"What do I care," I think. "I have eyes like Andy Garcia."

A Christmas Story

'm at the doctor's.

I'm sitting in the waiting room with about twenty other people. I have a long beard, a wool cap over my face, a fever, and red eyes. The room is infernally hot and dry, making me cough nonstop.

The others give me dirty looks like I've got the plague. The lady sitting next to me gets up to pretend to look for a magazine, then goes and sits somewhere else.

After about twenty minutes, the door opens and a man walks in. He's about seventy-five, shabbily dressed, disheveled, with dirty pants and an accent so thick it tests my own knowledge of my native tongue. As he's talking to the receptionist, I notice he has only two teeth. She looks at him with a mix of incredulity and disdain—as if he were homeless or something. The others share the receptionist's expression.

The man is holding a blue plastic bag with holes in it. The only clearly comprehensible thing he says is, "Is the doctor here yet?"

He goes on, like a chant: "Is she here yet? Is she here yet?" And the receptionist says yes, but he'll have to wait outside because she's busy at the moment.

But he persists: "Is she here yet?" pointing to the office door and giving the impression that he wants to go in now.

Some of the others start to look anxious; we're all waiting and some think the man wants to cut the line. At some point the man says something that sounds like: "Just a second, I just want to see the doctor for a second," and the receptionist says no, he has to wait. Outside, she says.

I say, if he wants, if it's really only for a second, I'll let him go before me. Everyone else in the room manifests their disapproval.

So he makes a slight gesture like "Fine, I'll wait." I stand up and let him have my seat. He sits down and flashes me a two-toothed smile. The young receptionist, who had imagined him waiting outside since all the seats were taken, gives me a dirty look.

Five minutes later, the man gets up and heads over to the reception desk again, holding his blue bag out to the woman. "You have to wait," she says. But he doesn't give up, holding out the bag with near urgency, saying he doesn't need an exam and can't stay but just came by to wish the doctor merry Christmas. The receptionist musters a close-lipped smile and says, "Ah." The man hands her the bag and goes out the door, telling everyone, "Merry Christmas, Merry Christmas," and smiling with his two teeth.

A heavy silence suddenly falls. The young woman sets the blue bag down and then switches it with a yellow bag that has no holes. For a moment, she empties the contents on the reception desk.

Inside the man's bag were two bottles of unlabeled wine, a discount panettone, and a little red flower.

Minestrina

I'm at the living room table inking a page. Ginevra is looking out the window.

"Daddy, why is the sun out if it's winter?"

"Ginevra, the sun comes out when it wants to; it's not like all winter it rains or there's only fog."

"But you said when the sun came out we would go to the beach!"

"No. Well, yes. But I meant when the summer sun comes out."

"And how long is it till summer, Daddy?"

"Six months, more or less."

She pauses. I can see her thinking.

"Daddy."

"What?"

"Is it six months before Sunday?"

"No, Ginevra, I didn't say six days, six months is a lot longer."

"Oh, good."

"Why's that?"

"Because Grandma's making me minestrina on Sunday."

God and Rapunzel

"Daddy, what's a Muslim?"

"Someone who believes in a God called Allah."

"Is he different from ours?"

"Yes and no, Virginia. Let's just say he wears different clothes."

"What do you mean?"

"How can I explain? You know how Ginevra dresses up as Rapunzel sometimes? She acts different and talks different, but you know that underneath she's still your sister. You know what I mean?"

"Sure."

Our Birthday

Today is our birthday.

Virginia turns eight, and Paola and I celebrate eight years as mom and dad.

Every morning when I wake her up for school and she climbs down the stool from her bed grumbling and leaps into my arms in the dark, my mind wanders back to me in my dumpy bachelor pad, when Paola took my hands and said, "There are three of us on the couch." I instinctively looked over my shoulder and thought, "That cat must have come through the window again."

That cat was Virginia. She wasn't behind me; she was inside Paola. Not over our shoulders, but in front of us, tracing our path together and establishing us as a family.

Never mind that we, by inclination, went with the flow, with no regard to last names. We're dreamers. We like surprises, and we never wanted stars guiding our journey, not even dancing ones.

It was always enough for us to follow the winds and trust in our own hands.

And in cats that come in through the window, especially them.

All for One

Two of our neighbors' houses got robbed the other night.

Yesterday after dark, Garrett was barking into the woods and I went to call him in. I thought it was the usual cat or maybe a boar, but instead I saw a shadow moving through the dark, illuminating its path with a small flashlight like one from a cell phone.

"Who's there?" I asked.

"I heard some noises," a voice said.

It was my neighbor from two houses down.

"Oh, I heard noises too, but it was you," I said.

He came up to the fence and told me about the other night. Two thieves were ransacking his garage, and upon hearing all the racket he went and looked in through the window. They saw him and ran away. He grabbed his air gun to scare them off with the noise, but his wife told him not to because he'd terrify the kids. They called the police, but in the meantime, the thieves escaped into the woods. Then they stopped for a second robbery at the yellow house at the end of the road.

Since Paola is away, last night I decided to sleep on the couch with the lights on. I barricaded the front door with the Chicco baby gate and kept a steel ladle handy, since a knife seemed excessive.

Around three, a violent noise woke me with a start. There was a monster movie on TV that, I must say, didn't make for a clear head. My heart started to pound. I picked up the ladle and listened. Another sound, this time from downstairs. I gripped the ladle tighter and put on my slippers. I went over to the spiral staircase and shouted, "Who's there?" Silence was the only response. Actually, as I later thought, it's unlikely that anyone would reply, "Robbers," but that's not how you think in the moment.

I opened the gate that was there to keep Melania from falling down the spiral stairs with a creak, and slowly descended. It must have taken me ten minutes to go down that staircase, one for each step. I could feel the ladle buzzing in my hand like a Jedi light saber. I hopped down the last step and swung the ladle in front of me, bracing for the worst.

In the cellar one of the dogs was closed up in the cot like a sandwich. The spring had given way and made it slam shut, and Garrett had gotten halfway stuck inside like in a bear trap. Cordelia was staring at him in the corner, sitting there perfectly composed. I freed Garrett and fixed the cot, and at that point, since I was there, I decided to take him out to pee so I wouldn't find any surprises to clean up in the morning.

As soon as I opened the door, Garrett ran outside barking, and Cordelia followed. It was three in the morning, so I rushed outside to get him. Garrett was at the fence barking toward the woods as if aliens were landing out there. I turned toward the trees and heard leaves rustling. I listened awhile and without a doubt, it was footsteps. I clutched the ladle, thinking how it would have been better to bring the wok too, but good ideas always come too late.

"Who's there?" I yelled into the darkness.

The footsteps came closer. I instinctively raised the ladle over my head.

"I heard a noise," my neighbor said.

"Damn it," I told him. "You nearly gave me a heart attack!"

The neighbor switched on his little flashlight and shined it in my face.

"Were you making soup?" he said.

"Oh, no, no," I said. "I just grabbed the first thing I found."

Then we heard more footsteps. We both turned around.

"Who's there?" we said in unison.

"I heard a noise," the second neighbor said.

When he came closer, we saw that he had fireplace tongs in his hand. The first neighbor, I noticed just then, was clutching a bicycle pump.

If we caught a thief, one of us could squeeze him, the second blow him up, and the third scoop up his tortellini.

The Man Who
Doesn't Laugh

This morning I saw a man digging through the trash.
I was dropping the girls off at school and all the
parking spots by the front were taken, so we drove
around twice, then parked up the hill. I left the car
near the yellow Caritas bins for clothing donations.
When I came out of the school and was walking back
to the car, I saw him. It's an increasingly common sight
in the city, but I'd never come across it out here.

Across the street, a husky guy in his sixties in a
dark green jacket was standing there watching the
man, with folded arms, his expression somewhere between surprise and mounting irritation.

"Go back where you belong and dig through the
trash there!" the guy shouted from the sidewalk, shaking his fist.

I didn't get that "where you belong" for a moment,
but then I realized that the man, whose face was almost completely covered by a red-and-white-striped
wool beanie and whose hands were deep in the bin,
was black. I was about to say something to the guy on

the other side of the street when a tiny old woman came walking down the street, leaning on a black umbrella as if it were a cane.

"What's your goddamn problem?" the woman shouted at the guy across the street. "You think he'd be digging through the trash if he wasn't poor too?"

The guy was dumbfounded, not having expected an outburst like that, and at that moment, the first man pulled a pair of old pink plastic clogs out of the bin. He looked at them, turned them around in his hands, and put them in a plastic grocery bag. Then he waved goodbye to the woman as if they knew each other and left without saying a word. I went up to her and wanted to hug her, but instead I just silently offered her my hand. The woman looked me up and down, suspicious. Then she shook it.

"These dickheads," she said, motioning to the guy across the street. "You should be grateful that life has gone so well for you!" she added, shaking her umbrella at him.

"Senile old bat!" the guy shouted.

"Your mama!" the woman replied.

It seemed like the guy was about to cross the street. But then, maybe because he saw me there, maybe because he realized what he was about to do, he came to his senses. He went off, hurrying up the hill and waving his hand in the air as if to say, "Both of you can go to hell."

"You should be careful though, ma'am," I told her.

"What do you mean, careful?" she said. "That fool? I've known him since he was ten years old. And he's always been a fool!"

I felt like laughing. I said goodbye to the woman, shaking her hand again, and went to my car and drove off.

When I got to the traffic light, I saw the man from the trash giving the pink plastic clogs to a ten-year-old girl.

The little girl was smiling, but the man was not.

Pockets Full of Stones

We've been sick the last few days.

Melania infected the entire family with a terrible virus that re-created scenes straight out of *The Exorcist*. We slept little, ate less, barely worked; we interacted in a haze, slowly and with increasing grouchiness. Ginevra and Melania have been home sick for five days, Virginia just succumbed this morning. She'd been jealous and difficult until today because she had been the only one going to school, and had to get ready in the morning without her sisters' company or Mama combing her hair. I'd yelled at her on more than one occasion, partly out of exhaustion.

Then last night, watching her in profile, a little lady sighing and finishing her homework, I remembered when she was a defenseless little pile of curls, and when she was two and knew *The Jungle Book* by heart and would flip through it and recite the text with a dubber's perfect timing while I secretly recorded her so I could try to convince my friends she already knew how to read. And now she's a schoolgirl—one day she likes one boy and the next day another; she has a poster of Marco Mengoni up next to her bed and pretty soon she won't even give me the time of day.

Being a father is brutal.

Your daughter will only be eight once and only four once and only two once, and every day, every hour, every minute you find yourself watching a series of shows with no repeat performances. You, from thirty-five to forty, have new experiences, you do stuff, but essentially feel like the same person. Whereas they, between two and eight, learn to speak, read, reason, develop tastes and form independent judgments. They *become*.

The thing you don't know is that it's not true that you stay the same person. Because while they learn life, you learn to be a father—that is, you learn your second life. What it means to stop being and start being present, to know that everything is going to fly by, to be able to catch that lucky smile that's all for you even when you're tired. The beauty of playing even if you're stressed, the wonder of those thirty-five pounds that want to do nothing but sleep on your chest even when you're dead tired and would give anything to sleep on your back without little fingers going up your nose. The fact is, your nostrils will be exactly the same in five years. Those little fingers won't. That desire to sleep on top of you will vanish too, and you'll regret every day you didn't enjoy it, every missed chance to rub that head when it was within reach. And when the show has moved on to other stages you can't see, when you're no longer in the front row but outside the door, you'll sleep on your back just to remember.

Being a father teaches you to focus, always. I know there are people who focus anyway, who don't have to have children to do that, and it's definitely a question of attitude and intelligence. A personal thing, as they say. But I, who have never shone with brilliance, only learned how as a father.

I used to waste tons of time; now I hoard it every day. I don't feel like an adult getting old while my daughters become young women; I'm more like a tireless wanderer filling his pockets with stones from the side of the road. Each of those stones is a memory that tells me that I was there. The stones slow me down and make me heavy, but each one anchors me to the present and makes me the foundation for someone else's future. That future is what I fight for every day, working even when I have a fever, losing sleep so I can be a pillow, letting every wall in my house be covered with scribbles because walls are just walls, while what makes a difference, at least for me, are the stones I'm able to carry along—for as long as my pockets hold up. When the stones fall to the ground, they'll be there for whoever may want to pick them up. Some perhaps in the form of iPad notes written at nine a.m.

before going downstairs to work; a coffee gone cold, left on the couch armrest while one daughter falls asleep with her head on my lap, while my back is still good and my pockets have plenty of room.

SPRING

The Moment Before

There's this thing. Spring is coming and I don't want it to.

The first baby birds are chirping in the yard and the crow has returned to the woods; at one p.m. yesterday it was 60 degrees in the sun.

I don't love spring, it's a cliché. The rebirth of life doesn't interest me, just the life that continues to quietly smolder beneath the ashes. I love waiting for the before, the latent potential, the pause that precedes the opening of wings, the promise contained by the cold. I've always been fascinated not by horoscopes but by astrological symbolism. My sign is considered the fixed water sign of the zodiac. Fixed water is the still water of a pond, as opposed to the running water of a river. I've always found it to be a perfect image, one that represents me to a T. Teeming life beneath a decaying, motionless surface, without a single ripple. Life you can't see but is there, that you don't suspect but exists. The tireless labor behind the trace of the visible.

Spring is life returning, brazen. Winter is life brooding, indomitable. Spring is the chick breaking through the shell of winter. Winter is the chick that dreams of its image as it gradually comes into being, taking its time, breathing under the snow, sensing but faintly the light of the world. The contrast between what is and the moment in which everything can still become.

The crossroads. Robert Frost just before he chose the road less traveled, stopping awhile at the inn at the edge of the woods, sipping a hot toddy and quietly planning his future.

The moment before the first step, in the first minute on the first day of the rest of the life you're about to choose.

The Blue Scooter

Ginevra and I are going down the stairs at the nursery school. We've just dropped off Melania.

At the bottom of the stairs, right outside the door, there's a blue scooter. Ginevra eyes it like it's a promise.

"Daddy, who do you think that scooter belongs to?"

"I don't know, Ginevra. It probably belongs to a boy who took his little brother to nursery school and parked it there."

"Did you know it was there yesterday too?"

"He must have taken him yesterday too."

We cross the yard. At the door to Ginevra's nursery school she stops and turns around.

"Maybe he's dead."

"I really doubt that, Ginevra."

"Well, how do you know?"

"Because scooters always go to heaven with their owners."

She eyes me, suspicious.

"Will your car go to heaven with you too, Daddy?"

"Well, yeah. Unless you want me to leave it for you."

"No, no, you can take it."

"All right."

"Just leave me a Popsicle and Mommy."

Love Can't Be Said

Paola doesn't know it, but I watch her.

I watch her while she sleeps, when she talks on the phone, as she writes.

She's radiant when she writes, even though she contorts herself into positions on her chair even weirder than a blind cormorant. Sometimes I peek at her reflection in the bathroom mirror while she's getting dressed, like in a romantic movie. Except I'm not lying half asleep between damp sheets like Richard Gere after making love. I do it on purpose, going between the bedroom and bathroom, to look at her.

Every day I add something to the image of the girl who put her hair up that July day, saying "Let's go," though I didn't know where. She was wearing just a pair of shorts and a tank top and in her eyes, she was only eighteen; maybe I was the same. Some days we still feel eighteen, and that's what saves us. I've clung to that image during the tough times, which we've had our share of. Because love is all in the eyes and nose and that's it. Sometimes in words. The rest is extra.

Anyway, I didn't want to say anything about love, because I think love can't be said, so I guess that's it. Except for one thing.

Once I read that a relationship dies if the couple doesn't grow together. That's not true. It doesn't have to be together. It dies when one doesn't recognize the growth of the other. The other's patterns and pauses. A couple is based primarily on patience, which is why so many people break up. Accepting that it is what it is, is devastating some days. You wish for something else, certain moments. Sometimes you almost feel like you're alone in the room and don't know where the other person went.

Paola and I, for example, often wait for each other. Sometimes I'm there, sometimes she's there, some days neither of us is. When we bump into each other like a couple of strangers waiting for the bus, those are the best moments, especially because the bus never comes.

Meanwhile, we've had three daughters, we create stories, we pay our mortgages, we laugh. We order a ton of pizza. We love each other in the cutouts, in the corners, in what's left over after everything else. Because, yes, a couple is the basis for a family, but like all foundations, it gets buried and you can't see it, to the point that you almost forget about it and it takes visionary faith to keep on *feeling* it. Paola and I have that in spades, and we've also got a few tricks: we still flirt with furtive glances in the hall; we meet like teenagers in the doorway between the living room and the bedroom and I want to take her in my arms, but she always has a full cup of tea in her hands. Paola hates it when I'm washing the dishes or breading meat when she wants to embrace me. Our embraces are out of sync. But it's actually all a subconscious tactic for making the unexpected ones even better.

Meanwhile I watch her reflection in the mirror, or as she writes. When she writes, she's radiant, even if she makes faces weirder than an albino iguana's. I also watch her while she sleeps and sometimes I make her turn over, because she snores like Popeye after a bender.

Last night though, sleeping alone because she was away, I was the one tossing and turning, for a long time. Without her snoring it's like being at a party after the music stops, eating the last little sandwich with a toothpick flag on top.

But she doesn't know that, so don't tell her.

Cashiers at Esselunga
Read Bukowski

The cashiers at Esselunga look at you with that self-righteous expression, knowing full well they're the only barrier between you and freedom.

They inspect your groceries like detectives. They deduce who you are by what you put on the conveyor belt, imperceptibly raising an eyebrow.

For years, the cashiers at Esselunga winked at me suggestively—when I looked like a young bachelor, rebellious but with the evident security of a real job. When I bought cases of Tennent's, artisanal Gragnano pasta, salmon and tuna for sushi, expensive coffee.

When I could afford those things.

Now, however, they look at me sadly. They note my plain clothes and discounted pasta, jumbo-pack diapers, baby food, and cans of formula with cruel pity. They remind me of swimmers at the beach looking at dirty seawater with resignation.

As soon as I pay, they shove my stuff to the side with that divider that looks like a giant nutcracker. Then they piteously toss me a couple of recyclable plastic bags, which invariably break before I get to the elevator.

Today something different happens.

The cashier at Esselunga, as I'm taking my things out of the cart, stares at me with gentle insistence. I'm not imagining it. She keeps looking up and over at me the whole time.

The cashier had to be thirty or so. Red hair gathered gracefully at her nape, milky white skin. Waxen. When our eyes meet, I don't know whether to feel flattered or uncomfortable. Maybe, I think, I have some trace of my charm as a faux melancholy suburbanite left. A patina that three daughters and sleepless nights and two mortgages and a lack of money have not yet managed to wipe away.

I bag the last things, my forty-year-old ego gratified.

"You're Mr. Bussola, aren't you?" she asks me out of nowhere.

I'm about to slide my card into the reader. I drop it.

"Um, yeah," I say.

I narrow my eyes and study her, trying to figure out if I can place her.

"I follow you on Facebook," she says bluntly.

"Oh," I say.

"You write very well," she says.

"Thank you," I say.

She pauses. She takes a breath as if about to confess a secret.

"Your writing really reminds me of Bukowski."

"Huh. You're really too kind. Anyway, I should say, I've stopped drinking."

She smiles. She doesn't know that I've just revealed a part of my life that few people know about. Maybe that's also why I don't know what to say next. I'm not used to talking to people anymore and my shyness has come back to claim its due.

"Sorry, but I really have to get going," I say.

I say goodbye, take my groceries, and leave.

Outside, it's about to rain. I unlock the car quickly and as I'm putting everything in the trunk, three thoughts come to mind, in the following order:

1. I was so bewildered by the situation that I didn't even ask her name.
2. If only I really wrote like old Hank, lady.
3. Against all stereotypes, cashiers at Esselunga read Bukowski.

That would make a great title for a story, I think.

I have half a mind to actually write it.

Being a Parent

I couldn't get to sleep last night.

I dug the remote control out from under the covers and turned on the TV. One of those late-night programs, where writers and scholars discuss a topic, was on. I couldn't tell what the topic was, but at some point someone I didn't recognize said something that rocked me.

He said it wasn't true at all that rubbing alcohol is a disinfectant.

You know, the kind in the pink bottle that our moms and grandmas put on our cuts or wiped on our skinned knees when we were little. Not only does it not disinfect, it's an irritant and even toxic. Skeptical, I went and looked it up on the Internet, and in fact he's right.

Which means, incidentally, that kids have been right for hundreds of years. When they cried, saying the alcohol burned, they were right. Besides burning, it's completely useless. But no one ever listened to them.

I found it to be a horrible realization, yet symbolic

and powerful at the same time. In an instant, I better understood the meaning of many things I've written.

Stories about my daughters or our road trips—and their funny, off-kilter view of the world—were perhaps an attempt to listen to them. To remind myself that my role as an adult and a father isn't to be right, but to acknowledge rightness when I see it. Not only to protect, but also to be protected. Not just to guide, but to let myself be led. To remind myself that children aren't right because they're children, but have a right to their childlike logic.

That the most important and difficult part of being a parent is perhaps being careful, always, not to burn our children's skin because of our fallible adult reasoning.

Spring Is Useless

In the car, on the way to nursery school:

"Daddy, why does spring only come once?"

"It doesn't only come once, Ginevra. It comes once a year, but it comes back year after year."

"Yeah. Spring is like Santa Claus."

"More or less, that's the idea."

"Except spring doesn't bring gifts."

"Well, that depends. The violets come out, for example. And primroses. And boars in the woods."

"And you can go to the beach."

"No, Ginevra, you know that you go to the beach in the summer."

"Geez, Daddy!"

"What is it?"

"Spring is useless."

April Fools'

had my first April fools' joke played on me in spring 1983.

Someone told me that the blond girl who sat in the back liked me. The blond girl's name was Vittoria and she was my second love. The first, Arianna, was taken away from me in fourth grade by her parents when they moved to another city.

I sent my friend Riccardo to check out the situation with Vittoria, because in any case, I didn't believe that she liked me and I was pathologically shy. I sent him to ask for definite confirmation. He asked her straight out: "Is it true that you like Matteo Bussola?"

I was bent on one knee outside the classroom door, pretending to tie my shoe. She saw me and gave me her answer, looking right at me.

"No," she said.

Riccardo came back to relay the message but I already knew. I got up and went to wait for the bus with a feigned laugh.

Antonio was in the courtyard; he was the one who told me: "April fools'! April fools'!" he sang at me.

I kept on laughing, since Antonio was two grades ahead of me and getting mad at him was prohibited. When I got home, my mom had made gnocchi. I ate less than usual and shut myself in my room. She came to ask me if everything was all right and I told her something bad happened at school. She understood immediately. That afternoon she gave me five thousand lire to buy a game I wanted, and letting myself go completely, I bought the Julio Iglesias tape *Che male fa innamorarsi alla mia età* a few days later.

Yesterday, while I was in bed waiting for the episode of *Force Five: Grendizer* to start, Virginia stuck a fish-shaped April fools' note on my back. "Turn around," she said. When she went off snickering, I removed it. The paper said: "I love Vittoria's mom." The Vittoria Virginia was talking about was one of her classmates. When I read the joke, it made me laugh a little. I went into the living room and there was Melania intently scribbling on the floor with a blue marker. I took it away from her and brought her into the bedroom with me. She climbed down from the bed and ran back to the living room, taking an orange marker from the box and resuming her writing on the floor. I cleaned it up this morning while making the three breakfast.

On the table was another April fools' fish torn in half with the words in pencil: "I love Daddy."

That's My Mother

'm at the pharmacy, there's a long line. Next to me there's a guy around fifty, well dressed, with a scarf carefully wrapped around his neck and hair like Conan O'Brien's. In front of us there's an old woman in a veil. He nods at me like, "See that?" I lift my hand like, "See what?"

"We're surrounded now," he says, indicating the woman in the veil and seeking complicity. He's not loud, but not quiet either; he says it without worrying whether the woman in front of us can hear. I feel like responding, "Yeah, by idiots like you."

Instead, I say, "That's my mother."

The veiled lady turns just slightly and smiles at me in profile. I relish the look on the guy's face, hanging between mounting embarrassment and that of a tourist in sandals who just stepped in elephant shit.

I wish I had a smartphone to take a picture of him as a reminder of the shitty country I live in.

But I don't, so I wrote this.

Boy Colors

This morning we saw the little boy with the blue scooter.

We passed him at the entrance when we were dropping Melania off at nursery school. We were walking in and he was coming out, his mom pulling the scooter by the handlebar. He was about eight, blond, with his hair short in front and long in back like German kids in the eighties. Ginevra watched him with suspicion and a touch of disappointment.

"Did you see that, Daddy? He isn't dead after all," she said to me on the stairs.

"Thank goodness."

"Otherwise, you know, his mom would be very sad."

"Right."

"And if he was dead maybe they wouldn't know who to give the scooter to."

"That's true, though blue is for boys."

She stopped on a step and looked at me.

"What is it?"

"Daddy. Colors are just colors, don't you know that?"

Then she went off again, giving me the cold shoulder and leaving me there on the stairs, with Melania in her little pink coat in my arms and a father's smile on my lips.

Beer Fest

Paola is at the store. I made a shopping list for her, item by item. She calls me.

"What's up?"

"Listen, I'm at the discount store and there's a sign that says, 'Beer Fest,' so I wanted to ask you if instead of the beer—"

"STOP! Don't take any kind of initiative! Get what I told you and that's it, please!"

"Geez, I was just trying to be nice, you know."

"Sorry, you're right. Okay, go on."

"Belgian beer is on sale."

"Uh-huh."

"There are two kinds."

"Okay. Describe the labels."

"One is white and one is yellow."

"Mm-hm."

"The yellow one says volume seven, the white one volume five. Which one should I get?"

I laugh.

"Listen, just leave them where they are. I haven't even read the first four volumes."

There's This Time

There's this time, perfectly balanced between afternoon and evening.

When the sun appears between the pines and the hill, the dusty light comes in through the window, the last rays cast long shadows on my studio wall and make the empty bottle of Franziskaner I use to hold paintbrushes sparkle. It all happens within a couple of minutes. The daylight fades slowly and I turn on the desk lamp, the dogs come back in from the yard to tell me it's dinnertime, I hear little feet running excitedly upstairs, Paola makes her umpteenth cup of tea, which she leaves in the sink or forgets on the bookshelf. I start to think about what to do for dinner while the brush slides over the paper, when the fiery sunset momentarily blends in with the lamp's electric light, as my hand grazes African faces and rocky landscapes that come to life between light and darkness, in perfect balance between the was and the will be, at the fork of the could be. Then the eye decides, the hand follows, the ink flows, the sun disappears behind the roofs of the houses, leaving a wake that starts out orange, then turns purple, then silver, then everything. Then nothing. Then night.

Chocolate Coins

In the kitchen, 7:30 a.m.

"Daddy."

"Yes, Ginevra?"

"You shouldn't go out this morning."

"Really?"

"Yes, you should stay home. You're sick and Mommy can take me to school."

"Well, if Mom agrees, that's fine."

"That way Mommy can start getting used to it."

"To what?"

"Taking me to school all the time, since she'll have to when you're dead."

"Ginevra, I really hope that by the time I die you'll be done with school and that you'll have had a driver's license for a long time."

"Okay, but if you want to die before then, don't worry, just tell me first."

"Thanks. If it does happen, I'll make sure to write you a note."

"Daddy!"

"What?"

"I don't know how to read!"

"Oh, right. What should we do then?"

"If you die, leave a chocolate coin on my pillow."

"All right."

"A big one!"

"Sure. How about, just to be on the safe side, I leave you two."

I have a coughing fit that lasts a good twenty seconds.

"Daddy."

"Yes?"

"Could you give me one now?"

Trail of Breadcrumbs

This morning I took the girls to school and gave them each two kisses, one for Paola and one for me. I went to the pharmacy and picked up two prescriptions, one for Paola and one for me. I went to the bakery and bought one plain croissant and one with jam, the first for Paola and the second for me. Then I went back home, made myself my third weak coffee and went down to my studio. I replied to two urgent e-mails, checked my bank account, prepared a paper square for a new page. The robin hit the glass like he does every day, because at that hour he sees his reflection in the glass door and starts a fight with himself. I opened the door and threw him some crumbs of pastry, but he got startled and flew away. Sometimes that happens with people too, I thought. When you open the door for them too fast, they get scared and run off. I sharpened a pencil and got to work with that thought in my head, I don't know why. The thought is still with me as I draw now, reminding me of two fears that decided to trust each other without running away, two doors that ended up becoming one. Behind that door there are breadcrumbs all over, and I like to think that they're the visible proof of the efforts we made to create a path leading home, like "Hansel and Gretel" in reverse. The house holds five lives and two paths, one for Paola and one for me. The two trails converge at one point—that point is here. Here begins a shared trail of breadcrumbs that fades into the horizon of a visionary faith, and it is renewed every day.

For Paola and for me.

Daughter to Go

The phone rings, there's no number.

   I chance it.

"Hello?"

"Good morning, hello. Mr. Matteo Bussola?"

"Yes, this is he."

"Hello, Mr. Bussola. This is Valentina from Sky Cable TV."

"Hi, Valentina."

"Mr. Bussola, I'm calling to offer you a new service that Sky is providing free of charge to its most loyal customers."

"All right."

"So, with the new Sky to Go service, you can watch Sky anytime, anywhere, even if you move or go on vacation, for example."

"Ah, I see. I'm not interested, thank you."

"How come? This is a very useful service, you know."

"Yes, but believe me, Valentina. One: I have no plan to move for, let's say, the next thirty years. Two: I never go on vacation except for a week at the beach in July."

"But it's free!"

"Okay. Tell you what. Try to convince me, I'll listen."

"Good. Imagine you're on vacation at the sea, like you said. But you don't have a TV. With Sky to Go you can access all Sky programs and services, even on the beach."

"On the beach?"

"Mm-hm."

"Sorry, but besides the fact that at the beach I usually read or get buried in the sand, if I don't have a TV, like you said, how can I watch Sky programs? With magic?"

"Well, on your enabled tablet or smartphone, obviously."

"Oh, so this is something for the telephone. Then that's no good, see? I don't have a smartphone."

"What do you mean you don't have . . ."

"I have a 2002 Nokia. It was given to me as a present after the Motorola broke, which had been given to me as a graduation present. It makes calls and nothing else and I'm perfectly happy with it."

"You don't have a tablet either?"

"Oh, like an iPad? Yes, yes, that I have."

"Well then, see?"

"Yes, but, correct me if I'm wrong: If I'm at the

beach, with my tablet and Sky whatever, I need to have a wireless plan, right? My tablet would have to be connected to a cellular network."

"Sure, obviously."

"Ah, well, that I don't have."

"What do you mean, you don't have that?"

"I didn't activate the cellular card for my tablet— the plan is too expensive for me. I only use my iPad at home, where it automatically connects to my home network."

"Excuse me, but what do you use it for then? The tablet, by definition, is a portable device. That's like having a cell phone and only using it to make calls from home."

"But portable is portable, right? In fact, we mostly use it in bed, to watch *Peppa Pig* videos on YouTube."

"Ah, perfect. You see? With Sky to Go you can watch *Peppa Pig* in bed on your tablet but through Sky, with access to many more episodes!"

"Yes, but I already have a TV in the bedroom. With Sky. So why would I need to watch *Peppa Pig* on Sky on my tablet when I can watch it on Sky on television? Also in bed, of course."

"Excuse me, but if you can already watch *Peppa Pig* through Sky on television, why do you watch it on YouTube on your tablet?"

"Because on Sky on the TV we watch *Dora the Explorer.*"

"Sorry, I don't understand."

"Valentina."

"Yes?"

"You don't have children, do you?"

"No."

"I didn't think so. Listen, I'll make you a deal."

"A deal?"

"Would you perhaps like one?"

"What?"

"Would you like one, a daughter? I'll send one right to your home. Free trial with no commitment."

"To my home?"

"Yes. She's portable, you know."

"But—"

"You can even take her to the beach, if you want. She works great at the beach even without a contract."

"Listen, Mr. Bussola—"

"I guarantee you that on the beach, if you take her there, you'll see things that Sky whatever can only dream of and you'll have full access to her shows. In high definition too."

"Have a good day."

"Wait, it's free!"

Click.

I didn't get a chance to tell her that there were even three different sizes to choose from.

Hopefully she calls back.

To Live—Forever
(Do the Dead Take
Their Cars to Heaven?)

This morning I was supposed to be on a train to Milan, but I'm not.

I'm almost happier, because this way, I was able to take the girls to school again.

On the way, we passed a hearse. Ginevra started to ask me what that strange car was, because it was all black and long. I tried to explain as best I could, but she didn't seem totally convinced.

"So dead people go to heaven in cars?"

"No, Ginevra," I said, "they go to heaven without them."

"Why do people die, Daddy?" she said later, out of the blue.

"Because that's how it is" was the only answer I could think of. "But fortunately, that goes for everyone."

She was silent for a long time, looking out the window. Then she resumed.

"Daddy," she said. "I want to live forever."

"Eh, well, you can't."

"Why not?"

"Because you can't."

"Yes, but why?"

I tried to think of an image to help her understand.

"Ginevra," I said. "Let's say life is like a pizza. We're all born hungry, and each of us is given a pizza. By living, we eat it a bite at a time, a slice every day. What matters isn't how big the pizza is, but only that in the end you're not hungry anymore. Do you understand what I mean?"

"I always get pizza with prosciutto," she said.

"That's true," I said, "and you always leave half because it's too much for you and you get full before you can finish. And so, what would be the point if they gave you a pizza that went on forever?"

She got quiet for a few seconds, then she looked at me.

"Daddy," she said. "Are you really hungry still?"

"Yes," I said. "I'd say I'm still pretty hungry."

"Well, what do you have on your pizza?" she said.

"The things I've chosen are on it," I said.

"Am I on it too?"

"Yes."

"And Mama too? And Virgi and Melania?"

"Of course."

"Well, on my pizza there's the whole world," she said, "because I'm only four years old."

Two Years

Today Melania turned two.

Her grandparents are coming over and I'm going to cook only things she likes. Rice with ham and peas, meatballs and potatoes, and we'll have chocolate cake. And I've been singing her "Happy Birthday" since seven in the morning, as a result of which she's now speeding around the house in her little red pajamas shouting, "To you! Too yooo!" with the same intonation as a sneeze.

I woke up before five a.m. to work on a few pages and make up for the time lost today on the party, since I have a deadline coming up next week.

"Lost" is an imprecise term, because all the time I've spent with Melania since she was born has always been time gained.

Truth is, I didn't wake up before five to get a head start on work, but because getting a head start on work allows me to spend more time with her.

And on this day, which is her day, it's twice as valuable.

Just like her two years, which are what give value and meaning to mine.

Can I, Daddy?

Getting into the car to go to nursery school:

"Daddy, can I bring some dandelions from the yard with me?"

"No, Ginevra, not in the car."

"Please! Just one!"

"No, because then you'll blow on them in the car like last time and the seeds will all get stuck to the seats."

"And they'll get our clothes dirty too."

"There you go."

As we're driving through the gate, she looks out the window.

"Daddy?"

"Yes?"

"Can I bring a blackbird then?"

Drawing for School

Virginia was making a drawing for school.

She'd been working on it for almost a week and was supposed to turn it in this morning. Last night, while we were on Skype with Mama in Milan, Melania snuck into Virginia's room, got up on the desk chair, grabbed a marker, and finished the drawing, covering the entire sky with big green spirals. Virginia was mad at first, then cried, then wanted me to write her teacher a note. I didn't, and after consulting Mommy, told her that unfortunately she'd have to redo the whole thing, because she was responsible for leaving it unattended near an uncapped marker—something we keep telling her she needs to pay attention to—and especially because, if she had focused on working instead of whining, she would have had more than enough time. She asked me for a sheet of the nice paper and in a huff began the drawing again at seven p.m. At eight we had dinner and afterward she went back to it. While I was in the bedroom watching a YouTube tutorial on how to braid hair, with Melania jumping on the bed and Ginevra watching cartoons, Virginia would come in and show me the intermediate steps, becoming increasingly confident. I encouraged her each time. She stopped around ten and went to bed with the sky half done. She finished her drawing before breakfast this morning, and ran to show it to me while I was dressing Melania. She had a gleam in her eye and an incredulous look on her face. The drawing was very meticulous. She wanted us to take a photo of it with the iPad and made me promise to send it to Mommy today.

"Daddy, it came out much better than last time. I'm almost glad Melania ruined the first one!" she said, filled with pride.

I was very proud too, because Virginia learned an important lesson today. She learned not to give up and how to react in a difficult situation without losing heart. That when they scribble on your paper and you have to start over from scratch, it's not always such a bad thing. That sometimes, when it seems like life is ruining all your plans, maybe it's just because it has something better in store for you.

But that something always depends on you.

The Hearts of Blonds

'm sitting in the waiting room at the doctor's office. It's full of people. I thought it would be, so I brought my iPad. I start writing to pass the time.

A blond girl has just sat down next to me. Around twenty-five, she's wearing an orange sweatshirt with ALOHA on the front and a flashy blue hat almost covering her eyes. She's chewing some kind of gum or candy that smells really good.

The girl sneaks a glance at what I'm writing, or at least it seems like she does. So I write, "The blond girl sneaks a glance at what I'm writing," and after two seconds I hear her laugh.

"I'm not sneaking a glance, my eye just fell there for a second," she says. "Also, I'm not blond."

"I wrote you were blond to muddy the waters and protect your identity."

"Protect it from whom?"

"You never know. Maybe I'll post it on Facebook and your father who doesn't know you're at the doctor will see it."

"It's true, he doesn't know."

"See? Now I'll even replace the orange sweatshirt with a turquoise turtleneck."

She laughs.

"What are you writing?"

"I'm writing a journal."

"Wow, that's great. Like in school. I always kept a journal too. Used to."

She says this with a look of irreparable regret, as if she were a thousand years old. She stares at the iPad balanced on my knees over the comic that Paola had brought me from the publisher yesterday.

"You read *Dylan Dog*?" she says.

"I'm one of the illustrators," I say.

"Really? No way! What's your name?"

I tell her.

"Sorry, I've never heard of you."

"I know, I know. It's just that my story won't be out until 2027, if I ever manage to finish it. Until then I'm incognito, so keep it to yourself."

She laughs.

"The latest stories are pretty good," she says. "I liked the last one a lot. The one that's really weirdly drawn."

"*The Heart of Men*?"

"Yes."

"Weirdly drawn is a great description."

"Sorry, I have a hard time expressing myself," she

says. "It's like you see the drawings and at first they seem bad. But after a while, you realize that's why they're so beautiful. I can't put it any better than that."

"I think you put it very well."

Suddenly the office door opens. No one comes out.

"Serughetti!" comes a voice from inside.

The girl leaps up and walks past me. She takes off her hat just before going in. She's completely bald. Everyone stares.

"I told you I wasn't blond," she says, turning toward me.

"That's okay. I don't draw for *Dylan Dog* either," I say, looking at her.

She laughs.

"Will you still put me in your journal? Even if I'm not blond?"

"Only if you want me to."

"I do," she says, and an instant later disappears into the office, the door shutting behind her.

The Tie

At the nursery school with Ginevra:

As I'm buttoning up her smock, another dad passes in front of us in a dark suit and tie, holding a briefcase in his right hand. He goes out.

"Daddy, why don't you have a tie?"

"Because I don't need one, Ginevra."

"But why do the other daddies have them?"

"Well, because they don't draw for a living."

"Why do you draw then?"

"Maybe because I don't like ties."

She looks at me seriously.

"Ties suck!"

"Exactly!"

"Daddy?"

"Yeah?"

"Grandpa got you an orange one at the market last Sunday."

Saving Yourself
Every Day

Every morning I get up at 5:05.
Technically, I wake up about fifteen minutes before, but I lie in bed with my eyes open. When the red digital alarm on Paola's nightstand says 5:05, then I get up.

I go into the kitchen, put the coffee on, then go down-stairs to let the dogs into the yard. I come back up, pour my coffee into the yellow elephant cup, and put five cookies on a small plate. I go back to my studio in the dark, trying not to kill myself on the spiral staircase.

I work from 5:05 until 7:05. I draw, immersed in si-lence; sometimes in the background there's the sound of Garrett snoring in the doghouse, other times there's classical music on Radio 3 that I put on low. Listening to music at a very low volume transforms the sound waves into a sort of primordial frequency, like a heart-beat. The melody fades into the background—it's vir-tually gone, and all you can hear is the drums, the percussion. The basses. The rhythm. That rhythm helps me to keep time while I work; it becomes the measure of the marks on the page, which in turn become the score for the vibrations I hear on the radio, which come from inside myself. Drawing is always a matter of tuning. Because drawing, like writing, is first and foremost about listening. Most people don't realize it's almost never a matter of saying, but of giving. Making yourself an instrument, a sounding box, for something which, upon closer inspection, is already there, and you just need to roll it out like a tent.

Every day I get up at 5:05. That's how it's been for years. I have a theory as to why.

The red 5:05, on Paola's clock, is in the typical square characters on digital clocks, and I always read it as: S:OS. *S-O-S*. In my imagination, it's a call for help coming from another dimension, like a message in a bottle cast into the open sea.

I know if I get up at 5:05, somewhere in the universe, I'm saving someone. Only recently did I discover that someone is me.

Waking up at 5:05, I save myself every morning, because the two hours between 5:05 and 7:05 are the most fruitful of the entire day. When the world starts up again, I'm already in a good mood, even if there's a crappy day on the horizon, because I feel like I've already finished a little of my own. As if every day pushed me a little ahead and my internal clock were two hours behind, giving me an advantage on the normal passage of time.

At 7:05, I go to wake Virginia. Then Ginevra. Finally, Melania. When I pull Melania out of the crib and hold her close and she rests her head on my shoulder, in the thirty seconds before I move her to the bed, into Mama's embrace waiting to snap her up like a shell, I save myself a second time, each morning.

The second time never happens at a specific hour, but that time is the one that counts.

The Dandelions

"All right, we're finally going to mow the lawn this afternoon. . . ."

"No, Daddy!"

"No?"

"No, if you mow the lawn you'll destroy all the dandelions!"

"Ah, Ginevra. What are we supposed to do? We can't exactly mow around them."

"Wait!"

"What?"

"I'll go outside and blow all of them, then when I'm done, you can go!"

Mommy Sleeps
All the Time

I n the car on the way to nursery school:

"Daddy, why does Mommy sleep all the time?"

"No, Mommy doesn't sleep all the time, Ginevra. It's just that sometimes Mommy has to work at night while we're sleeping. So sometimes she sleeps in, when we're already awake."

"Yeah, Mommy is like an owl."

I laugh.

"But can't she work during the day like you?"

"Well, sometimes she does. But she says during the day she gets distracted: the mailman comes, the phone rings, she gets messages, Grandma and Grandpa call, or I have to ask her things. But at night it's quieter and she concentrates better. And then in the afternoon she wants to be with you."

"Yeah, and she has to help Virgi with her homework."

"There's also the fact that Mommy prefers to work at night because she just likes it, I think."

"Daddy."

"Yes?"

"That way she doesn't see you at night."

The Boy Cartoonist

go out to get some paper.

At the stationery store, there's a little boy ahead of me. He's maybe ten or eleven. Skinny, not tall for his age, he's wearing a green Ninja Turtles T-shirt and lighter green cargo pants. His short hair is covered in sweat.

"And a putty eraser and a pad with rough paper," he says. "And a triangle, I need it for the panels."

The clerk disappears. The boy looks at me. I go up to the counter.

"Panels like in comic strips?" I ask. "Are you drawing a comic?"

He stares at me with a look somewhere between "how about you mind your own business" and "you ugly freak."

"Yeah," he says. "For school. Except I can't really draw."

"That doesn't matter," I say. "You know, to make comics, you don't have to draw that well."

Now his look is somewhere between "you're an idiot" and a flicker of interest.

"It's true," I say. "The story is what matters. Think about the story you want to tell and the drawing will come to you, you'll see."

He stares at me, unsure whether or not to trust me.

"I wanted to write a story about some shoes."

"Great," I say. "What shoes?"

"Shoes that when you put them on you know karate."

"Interesting."

"And then when you take them off you go back to normal."

"That sounds like a fine story to me," I say. "But be aware that shoes are hard to draw. Draw a kind without laces, trust me."

"I don't know how to draw laces."

"I don't know how to draw shoes."

"For me shoes turn out all right."

"Shoes only turn out for people who can draw," I say.

He smiles. The clerk hands him the bag; he pays, says goodbye, and leaves almost in a hurry. I see him through the window jumping onto his bike.

"He's a good kid," the clerk says.

"I'm sure," I say.

"And how can I help you?"

"Two pads of Fabriano F2 paper."

"Smooth or rough?"

"Rough. Now that I think of it, give me a triangle too, I need it for the panels."

The clerk stares at me, perplexed.

"I have to draw a comic," I say.

The Cookie

In the car on the way to nursery school:

We're backing out of the garage.

"Daddy, Daddy, are those stilts?"

"Huh? What?"

"Those things up against the wall."

"No, Ginevra. Those are storage racks."

"Racks?"

"They're rails, basically, holders. We use them when we go to the beach. They go on the roof of the car and we attach a big pod to them and put our beach stuff inside: umbrellas, water wings, beach chairs, toys, whatever."

"Daddy?"

"Yes?"

"This year at the beach I want to build a giant castle!"

"Okay."

"You have to remember to bring my shovels."

"Sure, Ginevra, don't worry."

"And then you need to get me some little flags."

"Flags?"

"Little flags to put on the roofs of the castle!"

"Ah. And what little flags do you want?"

"Castle flags."

"Yes, but what country do you want them from?"

"Huh?"

"What country?"

"Huh?"

"Do you want Italy, France, Spain, what?"

"Russia!"

"Russia? Why Russia? Do you like it?"

"I like the decorations on the houses in Russia."

"Ah . . . and where have you seen Russian houses?"

"I dreamt about them. And did you know they have tigers in Russia too, Daddy?"

"Oh, well, in some parts, yes."

"Daddy?"

"What is it?"

"This year at the beach, can we get the same cabin as last year?"

"Hmm, Ginevra. I don't know if we'll be able to get the exact same one. Every year it's been different— they have a bunch of bungalows all packed together and they give us whatever one they give us. In any case, it'll be basically the same, I promise."

"But I want that one!"

"Why? What was so special about it?"

"I hid a cookie in a drawer in my room."

"A cookie? Oh no, Ginevra, you left a cookie there a year ago?"

"Yes."

"After a year it definitely won't be good anymore, will it? It'll be really old by now."

A long pause.

"Yeah," she says. "Maybe it's dead."

To do for this year's beach trip:

1. Giant sandcastle
2. Find little Russian flags
3. Cookie funeral

The Snake

I went to take out the trash and saw a snake.

A whip snake, I'm sure. Not too long, a baby I think. It was in the street.

Knowing our neighbors, I realized it was doomed. So I did something that before Paola, I never would have done even if I'd lived a thousand lives: I went inside, put two rubber gloves on one hand, grabbed the fireplace tongs with the other, and went out.

The snake was still there, almost in the same spot. I approached slowly, breathing hard, and in a flash caught it by the tail. It jerked in fright and started to wriggle and coil as if it were having an epileptic fit. I nearly lost it because for an instant the idea crossed my mind that it might be another kind, since I know about as much about snakes as I do about soccer. Running like an old man with a fishing rod being chased by a murderer, I got to the woods in two seconds flat and tossed it in a bush.

Then I went back into the house, googled "heart attack symptoms," and after a few minutes, "how to catch a whip snake."

Never catch it by the tail, it says. Because "if you do and you don't keep their head still with your other hand, they can give painful bites."

There you go, by dumb luck I'd come upon the only lazy whip snake in the Veneto.

Anyway, it's like they say: it takes one to know one.

The Hairband

Yesterday, Virginia asked me, "Daddy, if you and Mommy break up, who will take two daughters and who will take one?"

I was slicing onions in the kitchen. The question took me by surprise.

"What do you mean, Virginia?"

"We're three sisters," she said. "You obviously can't cut the third sister in half!"

I felt like laughing. I was about to say, "Don't worry honey, Mama and I will never break up," but I didn't want to lie. I know relationships are reinvented day by day, and the worst mistake you can make for yourself, or for others, is thinking you're invincible.

"Virginia," I said, "if for some reason Mama and I separate one day we'll both see all three of you, sometimes me and sometimes Mama, don't worry."

"But in *Mrs. Doubtfire* the dad only saw the kids on Saturdays," she said.

"Virginia, sometimes when parents break up things can happen," I said. "Maybe they didn't separate on good terms and fought. But Mama and I agree that, even if we leave each other, you three will always come first. Understand? Always."

She stared at me silently.

"Daddy," she said after a while, "does love end?"

I thought for a second before responding.

"Love never ends," I said. "It's people that change."

"People?"

"Virginia, adults grow too, you know? You're a big girl now, but seven years ago you were a baby. It's kind of like that for mommies and daddies too. When I met Mama I was a different person, so was she. The important thing when two people love each other is to be able to change together, or respect the other person's changes. That's what parents do with their children, but between themselves sometimes they can't. That's why love for your children is the only kind that never ever ends."

"But," she said, "when you met Mommy how did you know she was Mommy?"

"I don't know what you mean."

"How did you know you loved her?"

"Oh, that," I said. "I knew that after about ten minutes."

"How?"

"The first time we met, she pulled her hair back behind her neck, lifted it up over her head, and put it into a bun without a hairband, just twisting it in a knot."

"So what?"

"So I knew she desperately needed a hairband. And I needed her hair."

"And did you have a hairband?"

"No, but by the time Mama found that out she already loved me."

"Daddy," she said, "that means you tricked her!"

"Maybe just a little," I said, "but the point is Mama was the first woman who ever made me want to find a hairband, you know what I mean?"

She looked at me for a few seconds.

"Here, Daddy," she said, pulling out her hairband. "Now you and Mama won't break up."

She laughed, and fortunately I was slicing onions.

SUMMER

The Right Way

last night I heard a noise.

It was four a.m. and we were sleeping with the window open. I got up in the dark, put my T-shirt on inside out, and went into the hall. I turned on the bathroom light so I could see and went into the girls' room. Ginevra was sitting on the edge of her bed, her knees tucked under her chin.

"Daddy," she asked, "would you bring me some cold water?"

She handed me a bottle, I ran the tap in the bathroom, emptied the bottle and refilled it. I sat next to her, she drank it, asked me to fix her covers, and then went back to sleep. By then I was awake, so I went into the kitchen. I got a focaccia and a coffee and went down to the studio and into the yard. As I drank my coffee in the dark, sitting on the wall, I collected my thoughts—the usual things for a forty-year-old father: money problems, drumming up work every day, how I'd like a new computer. You feel more forty at four in the morning. At that hour, you can turn around and catch sight of a few small regrets that seem bigger in the dark, or a handful of good memories that break your heart. Then I noticed that the apricot tree we'd just planted was a little dry, so I filled a bucket with water and gave it a drink. It was in looking at the tree that I remembered something. I remembered that five years from now we'd be eating apricots from our garden. I remembered that because for a second I had the perspective of a fifty-year-old man looking back; he remembers the apricot tree, he remembers with a twinge of melancholy what the first fruit was like and how the girls smiled. Or maybe not—maybe the apricot tree will die and become a sad memory. But now, sitting on the wall in the dark, I thought, I'm a forty-year-old looking ahead. The tree is here and still needs to grow. I look at it and I don't see regrets, or memories, just a goal. It makes me think of this image of a crowded one-way street with a man waiting to cross at the crosswalk. The image leads to a thought. The thought is that, what matters, when you venture into the street, whether you're behind the wheel or crossing on foot, is just remembering to look the right way.

Nothing Happens

Paola is at her parents' with the girls, I'm supposed to go to the store.

I go down to the yard and open the gate, say "hi" to my neighbor pulling weeds in his garden. I get in my car. I turn the key in the ignition and nothing happens. I try again. Nothing happens. I try again. The starter makes a rattling sound like gangsters do in films when they get shot and have some crucial truth to reveal in a friend's arms before dying. My truth is that my battery is dead. I consider my options: I could call the mechanic and have him come all the way here to jump the car, but the service charge alone would be twenty euros. Or I could wait—since Paola has the cables in her car and they're coming back the day after tomorrow, it would only be forty-eight hours. In a surge of bucolic enthusiasm, I tell myself, "Why not, the supermarket's only three kilometers away, and I just need a few things, it's no big deal." I grab the yellow shopping bag, get out, wave again to the neighbor in the garden, who'd been looking at me the whole time like "you know it'll go faster if you turn it on," and set off.

On the way, the road is downhill. For the first kilometer, I feel like I'm in a Gene Kelly movie—there's even Gershwin in the background. Halfway through the second kilometer, I start getting hot. Halfway through the third, I feel like Vince Vaughn in *True Detective* in that scene where he crosses the desert on foot after getting stabbed. When I walk into the supermarket, my light green shirt is now dark green. I lock eyes with a new, cute young cashier with a braid, and I can't help but think how from now on, she'll always remember me as That Sweaty Old Guy, but I trust the words KING OF COOL on my T-shirt will make her see me as the master of self-irony. I throw some lemons in my basket and continue to the meat section. There are six-pack chicken legs—why not. I get a bag of parmesan, a box of spaghetti, some ice cream. A tin of anchovies. Then it happens: I see "discount" in proximity to "beer." The discount ends today. I consider how the walk home will be three kilometers uphill; how I already risked emphysema on the way, downhill and without any extra weight; but in my head a voice like the drill sergeant in *An Officer and a Gentleman* yells at me, "Private Bussola, stand straight in that mud!" I put five tallboys in the basket, well . . . let's make it six. An extra can of "Beer"-brand beer—hey, you never know. I head to the checkout. I fill my yellow grocery bag and pay.

When I get outside, the eleven a.m. sun kisses my forehead as if making a promise. The promise says, "I'll go get some popcorn." I walk like the zombie in *Cemetery Man* dragging a corpse. After the first bend in the road I can't feel my right arm. After the second, I can't feel the left. After the third, I can't feel anything. The beers clink together in the bag, cruelly mocking me. In a stroke of genius, I try to put the bag around my shoulders like a backpack; I desist only after risking strangulation for the fifth time. When I pass a blue Ape truck for a second I think of throwing myself like dead weight onto the cargo bed, but in my head Sergeant Foley's voice shouts, "There's only two things in the Veneto, cattle and conservatives!" And in a surge of bovine pride, I pull myself together. When I'm about halfway up the hill, I decide to stop and catch my breath for a moment at Marisa's bar, might as well. Marisa isn't here today; her daughter is at the bar. I ask if she can keep my ice cream in her fridge while I sit down. I order a small beer, but instead, she comes back to me with a medium lager, saying "this one is new—you have to try it, you drink it with pepper!" With pepper. How about with a loaded nine millimeter, I think to myself, but can't bring myself to say it out loud. I set off again and finish the rest of the trip in a Salvador Dalí painting. In front of me, through the beads of sweat clouding my eyes like cataracts, I see only melting clocks, trees reaching out to grab me, flying tigers coming out of the mouths of clownfish with vampire teeth. With less than half a kilometer to go, I see Francesco Moser skateboarding past me. I make the last three hundred meters on nothing but sheer Veneto will. Once my house is in view I'm all one color—even my green shirt has turned maroon. My neighbor with the garden looks at me from his balcony, I nod at him like, "Relax, even doctors recommend getting a little exercise. . . ." I open the gate, take fifteen minutes to get up the stairs, and roll onto the couch, groceries and all. My eyes close as the voice of announcer Nando Martellini echoes in my head shouting, "World Champions! World Champ—" Then they open suddenly. I realize I left the ice cream at Marisa's and forgot to buy butter.

I consider my options.

I guess I'll prepare a sorbet out of green apple hand soap and attempt to make margarine out of curdled basil.

Four

All four of them are back home whereas I'm down in the studio working, keeping an ear out. They had gone straight to bed.

One I put to bed without pants. One without her teddy bear. One without a sock.

One without me.

The Cat

Melania doesn't just say "A!" anymore.

Now she also says "es" to mean yes, and the one time out of ten when she gets the "y," she says "yesh" and bursts out in applause. She also calls cartoons "boo-boos." And says "mo!" for more. More what is a mystery—it could be more water, more fries, or "Pick me up, old man, can't you tell I want to lie on your chest some more? Learn to talk, why don't you."

The only comprehensible word she pronounces (almost) correctly, the only unmistakable word that has climbed to the top of her highly personal top five loves, even ahead of Mama, is "Cake-uh."

"Cake-uh" means any sweet, from candies to muffins to chocolate eggs to pudding. But the ultimate "cake" remains the undefeated discount store Danishes. The discount Danish, or "Danish"-brand Danish, is straw yellow, and when you take it out of the package, you get a whiff of hay and honey and cream cheese. It comes in a light blue package that makes it look like the little cracker packets they give you in the hospital. I have to open it for her, but without throwing away the wrapper, which has to remain in sight. Then I have to peel it off the little paper boat that serves as internal packaging without taking it all the way out. She grabs it, bites into it on one side with her big hook tooth, and then meticulously crumbles it up into about a hundred pieces. When she's done with that operation, she puts all the crumbs together and throws them into her mouth like confetti on Mardi Gras.

After finishing her "cake," Melania looks at you and bites off your nose. The nasectomy has evolved from what it used to be. Now it alternates between: "Give me some water," "I want a pound of chips on the little elephant plate," "I want a chunk of parmesan, no, some prosciutto, actually two hot dogs," "Take me out of the high chair, I said take me out of the high chair, I-said-take-me-ooooout!" "All the markers here, now!" "Where are my darn toy pots?" and "I'll have a cutlet and French fries on the side, thanks."

When she bites my nose and laughs, it means she's really happy. When she bites my nose and laughs, I'm really happy too.

When she falls asleep on my belly at night, just after dinner, I eat the crumbs from the cutlet or Danish off her like a cat licking her kitten clean. Then I lift her a little and whisper in her ear, "Should we go to bed, Melania?" And she lifts her head a little without opening her eyes and says to me, "Yesh."

I get up, holding her tight, and we head quietly down the hallway. I lay her gently in her crib, straighten her legs, and rub her head. Getting to her bedroom door ends the best half hour of my day, every day. With a pang of nostalgia that gets stronger every night; with drool on my sweatshirt, always in the same spot, which by now seems intentional; and a bad craving for Danish-flavored cutlet that I hope never goes away.

Cyrano

The first time I broke my nose, it was my twelfth birthday.

It was a middle school party, my party. The attic, with the strobe lights and the blue and red spotlights and the egg cartons on the ceiling for soundproofing, was all decked out. We'd worked on it long and hard, we'd hung posters of Gazebo and Spandau Ballet and the Police on the wall—it seemed like a real home discotheque.

I was dancing with Lara, who I knew liked me. I also knew that my friend Riccardo—whose house it was—had a huge crush on Mariarosa. What Riccardo didn't know was that Mariarosa was dying for him to ask her to dance. It wasn't obvious; Lara had just revealed it to me. Looking past her hair, I observed the two: Riccardo with his unbearable hesitation and Mariarosa with her hopeful suffering.

When "Careless Whisper" came on, it was time—I said to Lara, "Just a second," and I ran over to my dumb friend, with a clear idea of what I needed to tell him. Something like, "If you don't ask her *now*, I'll never let you copy my history homework ever again."

I was only a few feet from him when I ran into his brother. He was fifteen, a head taller than me, with his shoulder and torso in a cast from recently breaking his collarbone. In the intermittent half-darkness of the attic, my face slammed into his cast like a Fiat 500 into a brick wall. I fell back and passed out, waking up in my own blood.

When I came to, Riccardo still hadn't danced with Mariarosa. On the bright side, now I looked like Owen Wilson. They took me to the emergency room and everything, but it was the early eighties, and in those days you were stuck with whatever you did to yourself as long as it wasn't life-threatening. So my nose remained.

Seven years later, I broke it for the second time during a karate match. Filippo knocked my guard off with a textbook *ura mawashi geri* that hit me right in the face and sent me flying. When I fell onto the mat I heard the distinct pop of nasal cartilage. Back at home, with my white karate uniform looking like the Japanese flag as painted by Jackson Pollock, my mother told me, "Maybe you should stick to cycling."

But before I had the time, I moved to Venice.

There, during my first university party, I slipped on

a bridge—too much ice and vin brulé—and fell face-down on a step. That was the third time I ruined my nose, even if I didn't really realize it until the next morning, waking up at some blond girl's place off Campo delle Girandole.

The fourth and last time was eleven years ago.

I'd just met Paola, but we hadn't gone out yet. We were still at the stage where we were just writing to each other and she considered me a harmless schmuck, due to my abundant use of emoticons.

On a June night during that period, at a popular bar in Verona, someone made an offensive wisecrack to my friend Silvio. I'm very protective of my friends and I responded directly with my innate and reaction-ary . . . *ahem* . . . expressive abilities. The guy took it partly as a joke, partly not, and mimed a head butt in my direction. He did it so well that he tripped and crashed right into my nose. After a half hour of lack-luster blows, we were drinking gin and tonics together on the stairs. He told me he was epileptic and asked for a cigarette. I gave him one, he sniffed it deeply and then tucked it behind his ear.

"Sorry again about your nose," he said.

"What happens if you have a seizure when you're drunk?" I said.

"I stay drunk," he said.

"Ah, there you go," I said.

I went back home with a swollen nose and at two in the morning I wrote Paola.

It was the first time she wrote me back immediately.

A week later we went on a date.

There Are Lots of Love

While we were in the car this morning, Ginevra asked me about love.

"Daddy," she said, taking me by surprise, "can two women get married?"

Before answering I thought hard; I really wished Mama were there in my place.

"No," I said, not wanting to lie to her. "Here they can't, but they can love each other and live together."

"Like you and Mommy?" she said.

"Yes."

"But why can't they get married?"

"It's a complicated issue, Ginevra," I said. "In some places they can, but they can't here yet."

"Can they do it in Sant'Ambrogio?"

"No, Ginevra, not anyplace. I meant countries, like Italy."

"But I saw two girls kissing in Sant'Ambrogio."

"There's nothing wrong with that, Ginevra. If they love each other very much, everyone can kiss."

"Even boys?"

"If they love each other very much, yes."

She paused, and it seemed like she was gearing up for something.

"Daddy," she said, "when two women get married, how do they love each other?"

"The way everyone in the world does," I said. "With their heart."

"Love is inside the heart?"

"Everything is inside the heart."

"Why?"

"Because the heart is like a big closet, Ginevra," I said. "Inside are the people you choose, and there's a shelf for kisses, drawers for hugs, hangers for looks, a row of hooks for sadness and for happiness. Everything."

"Melania has a drawer for food on her face!"

"True," I said, laughing.

"Daddy," she said.

"What?"

"There are love in our hearts, right?"

"Yes, but you don't say 'there are,' Ginevra. You say 'there is'; love is singular."

"That's not true!" she said, looking serious. "There are lots of love."

I shut up and didn't correct her any further, because I believe there are lots of love too.

The Courier

Early Saturday morning, I'm down in the studio, when the doorbell rings.

I go and see who it is. It's a courier with a package. The courier is a strapping young man with a pointy beard and a Spider-Man hat. The package, judging by its size, looks like a book, and I think I know which one.

"Paolo Barbato?" the courier asks.

"Paola," I say.

He gives me a strange look.

"Paola is my wife. Well, she's not actually my wife, but anyway, the package is for her," I say.

"And how do you know who the package is for?" he says.

"Excuse me, but you just told me yourself," I say.

"I told you it's for Paolo Barbato," he says.

"Yes. And I told you there's a mistake, the name is Paola Barbato," I say.

"It's Paolo written here," he says.

"But it's actually Paola," I say.

He stands there in front of me hesitating, holding on to my book. He stares at me, perplexed. I'm in my undershirt, it's chilly, and I want to go back inside.

"Fine then, that's me," I say.

"You're Paolo?" he says.

"Yes," I say.

"Why didn't you say so to begin with?" he says.

"I'm embarrassed, I don't like the name," I say.

He looks at me questioningly. He passes me the electronic thingy and stylus through the closed gate.

"Sign here," he says.

I sign. He delivers me the package. I smile at the electronic thingy.

"Who's Matteo Bustolo?" he says.

"Bussola," I say.

"Who's Matteo Bussola?" he says. "Weren't you Paolo Barbato?"

"Listen," I say. "The package contains a book. If you want, I can guess the title without even opening it. On the bell it says 'Bussola-Barbato.' So who do you think Matteo Bussola is?"

He looks at me strangely.

"Your wife?" he says.

Five Scars
(The Habit of Staying)

have five scars.

One I got tumbling down the stairs at the age of three. My chin hit a corner hard and split open. Every so often Virginia says to me, "Daddy, can I see the scar under your beard?" I lift my chin and she digs through my beard and looks at the scar, then asks me if it hurts.

The second is on my chest, the result of a long operation after my lung exploded one summer night. I slept on it all night thinking it was just a pain between my ribs, but it was one of my lungs that had collapsed on my heart. I survived due to a mixture of intuition and good timing and because the second doctor took me seriously instead of sending me home with two tablets of Voltaren like the first one did.

The third scar is in the middle of my right hand, from a cut I got when I was young and too stupid to realize that sometimes you actually win when you lose.

The fourth and fifth aren't visible, but they're the only scars that still hurt.

I didn't learn anything from the first three, but from the others, I did.

I learned that when things end it's not necessarily your fault, but if you try to protect yourself by keeping others at a distance, you can't expect to get them back when you feel ready all of a sudden. That life is what happens, even if it's made of what you choose. And with what happens, you generally have two choices: embrace it wholly or walk away.

For a long time, I thought I wanted to be free like a sailor about to set out to sea. But now I know the freedom I choose and the strength that counts—that horizon I thought I would have to keep searching for farther and farther away—don't come from the inclination to leave.

But from the habit of staying.

Dinner

Dinner at our house:

I set some meatballs in front of Melania. "Nyo!" she says, pushing the plate away and eyeballing her sister's grilled cheese.

"Meto! Meto!" (Translation: Me too, now! You're trying to starve me!)

Virginia offers half her sandwich in pity. Melania crumbles it up into three hundred and seventy-seven pieces, sees there's prosciutto inside, sucks on it, gets down from her seat, and runs away. Paola gets up too.

"Where are you going?" I ask. "I can go after her, I'm afraid she'll jump off the balcony." But Paola runs to get her anyway.

"*Three olives inside and five on the side*, I said!" Ginevra yells at her sandwich. Then she looks at me with a hand already in the toy make-up and a fuchsia eye and says, "I'm gonna make myself pretty!" Then she gets up and leaves.

Virginia abandons her sucked-on cube of cream

cheese and half sandwich and says, "I hafta go pee-pee!" And she too goes off. That makes four.

I stay at the table by myself for about fifteen seconds in a banquet of leftovers, with the same deep sense of solitude that Bill Murray had in the Suntory whiskey commercial. I toss a drooly half sandwich in my mouth; compose a ball of cream cheese, bread crumbs, prosciutto fat, and lettuce and throw it down the hatch; and clean up as I finish chewing. I go back and scarf down Melania's meatballs, squirting a little mustard in my mouth right out of the container, as I watch the end of the *Peppa Pig* episode with Grandad Dog and the boat.

And they say gastritis makes you introverted.

The Tickles

Ginevra and I woke up at five a.m. today.

Yesterday she threw a tantrum about going to sleep and kept whining intermittently throughout the night. First she was hot, then cold, then thirsty, then itchy. Around four-thirty she started complaining that her feet hurt. When I was little I too had bad foot aches, which peppered all the visits to all the museums of European Art with complaints, to the delight of my father, who always thought I was exaggerating. And so I took her feet in my hands and rubbed them for a while. It was useless because Ginevra laughed, saying it tickled.

By then we were both awake and it was pointless to force her to go to sleep, so we both got up, got dressed in the bathroom, and went into the living room. We flopped down on the couch and watched cartoons while we munched on cookies. Ginevra was very happy, because there were different cartoons on at that hour from the later morning ones. The previous night we'd forgotten to close the shutters and there was a faint light, like when you'd wake up early to go to the beach when you were little. It was the first dawn we'd seen together since she was born. Ginevra was wearing her new sky-blue Peppa Pig T-shirt and petted it as if it were a puppy.

At some point she turned to me and said, "Daddy, do you want to wake up together every morning, just us two?"

I smiled because I knew that waking up at this ungodly hour, she'd go to sleep at nine tonight and then I'd have to wake her up with a cannonade the next morning so she could visit her grandparents in the mountains.

"Maybe, we'll see," I said.

That was when Virginia stormed into the living room all disheveled and sweaty, saying, "Did you forget about me?"

And Melania woke up in her crib singing a vowel-only version of "Twinkle, Twinkle, Little Star."

I went into the baby's room and picked her up and rested her sweaty head on my shoulder. Virginia went to the bathroom to brush her teeth. Ginevra asked for a muffin, and while I was giving Melania her milk, Ginevra looked at me with grown-up complicity, as if we shared a secret.

In the car on our way to the store, she took off her sandals and poked her feet a little.

"Daddy, my feet don't hurt anymore, you know," she said.

"Great," I said.

"But I still have the tickles," she said. "And I feel like laughing."

In the rearview mirror I saw her and Melania chewing on a piece of tart that had been on the seat since Saturday.

"Me too," I said.

Toi, Tu La Connais?

A French comics editor I haven't heard from in about a year writes to me.

The gist of the conversation, in thick French, is more or less as follows:

"*Oo-la-la*, profiterole! I tell you I get back to you, *n'est-ce pas?*"

"*Allez-allez*, with calm, eh. Don't wear yourself out."

"Listen, so, since in practice we have not yet found someone, would you like to do a sample for this *projet*? That is, clearly, I'm asking you *pourquoi* we truly, truly thought of you right away, eh?"

"A-ha-ha, *merci*. I'm happy you thought of *moi*, but at the moment, *je suis* busy with another sample and with an *Italien* book. . . . Are you in a very big hurry?"

"Did you say *Italien*? Do you mean to compare an *Italien projet* with an *internationale* proposal from our *très grand* publishing *maison*?"

"No, *moi*, I didn't want to compare them, I'm just busy at the moment, that's all."

"For how long?"

"Eh, how long, the rest of the year for sure. At the very, very least, eh?"

"So I should take this as a 'no, *merci*'?"

"Eh *oui*, sadly."

"You stupid *Italien* loser!"

"Ta soeur!"

"Excusi?"

"My regards to your sister."

"Toi, tu la connais?"

"In Italy, everyone does."

Dog Eyes

Paola always told me I had dog eyes.

Dog eyes are eyes with a slight droop that, regardless of situation or expression, give off a hint of vague and indelible melancholy that the unobservant mistake for depth; but actually, I know it's supposed to be a compliment because Paola loves dogs more than anything. But every time I think of it, I laugh—it makes me think how sometimes we might believe we're falling in love with someone because they're sensitive, or beautiful, or sweet, or because they meet our needs or show up at the right time. Whereas things happen like someone falling in love with you because you have dog eyes, or because when you laugh you get just one dimple, on the left. And you with her because she has round ears like a cartoon character. Or because every time you see her laugh, you get just one dimple.

On the left.

Miss Marisa

I left without having breakfast this morning.

The fact that the two older girls are in the mountains put me off schedule, and I found myself in the car realizing that I hadn't even had any coffee. So I said to myself, "Screw it," and stopped at Marisa's to get my fix with a double espresso and a croissant. When I got out of the car, I saw Marisa in the doorway, cleaning intently, broom in hand, the place deserted and the shutters halfway down. I suddenly remembered the bar is closed on Mondays.

"Come on, come in anyway," Marisa told me. "You can keep me company."

She had me sit down and brought me a cream-filled croissant and some apricot juice, since the espresso machine was off and—even though she offered—I didn't have the heart to make her turn it on just for me. She sat in front of me with that look of knowing weariness shared by all women of that generation and all mothers over sixty. She told me her life story for the hundredth time, how she raised three children by herself, how she managed to buy the bar after working as a housecleaner, a cobbler, a produce seller, and finally a factory worker at a big plant in the South for ten years. An internal emigrant in reverse.

As I finished the delectable croissant, ready to ask for another, shooting lustful glances at the cabaret of delights on show at the bar, a thought came to me.

"Marisa," I said, "how come you have croissants and pastries even when you're closed?"

"Eh, partly out of habit, partly because the baker is a dimwit who doesn't understand squat," she said. "It doesn't matter, anyway."

At that moment, a young black man with a pile of bags almost as tall as he was entered the saloon, making an entrance like John Wayne. He came into the bar without ringing or anything, as if it were his house. Immediately I thought, "Here we go, we're about to witness the usual tragedy of 'I don't need anything, go away, we're closed,' at the very least."

"Marisa!" the black man burst out. "Have you seen what a nice day it is?"

"Yeah, be happy it's not pouring on your head anymore, honey," Marisa said, standing up.

The black man set his bags on the ground, zipped one open and pulled out a cardboard box full of different-colored lighters, like the little Bics.

"What'll it be today?" he asked her.

"Hmm. All right, give me orange," Marisa replied.

Marisa took the little lighter, looking the black man up and down, and set it on a shelf next to the bar that had, I swear, like fifty lighters in all different colors. Then she lifted the pastries in plain view, put some in a paper bag, added a bottle of mineral water and handed it all to the young man. He smiled, displaying a row of bright white teeth, took the bag with the pastries, loaded the bags up on his back again, thanked Marisa, and slid out the door without even asking me if I wanted to buy anything.

"Don't eat them all at once, Mamur!" Marisa shouted behind him.

Mamur waved goodbye, already biting into the first one.

Marisa came back and sat by me, immediately noticing my inquisitive look.

"Eh, you can never have enough lighters," she said, shaking her head.

"Right," I said.

Then I felt a tic in my left eye like when I'm about to cry, and Marisa asked me if I wanted another juice, but I said "No thanks, I need to get going."

Above the Clouds

Ginevra called me from Grandma and Grandpa's cabin in the mountains.

"Daddy, did you know the sun's out here?"

"I'm glad, peanut. Here it's a little foggy."

"Why not here?"

"Because up there you're above the fog; it's like you're above the clouds."

"Come on, Daddy, the clouds are in the sky!"

"Right, I meant that if the fog was a cloud, you'd be up even higher."

"Daddy, what would happen if I jumped on a cloud?"

"You'd fall, because clouds are made of vapor."

"And if I jump on the fog?"

"Fog is just like the clouds—you can't jump on it."

"Geez, Daddy."

"Ginevra, it's not my fault. If you can't, you can't."

"Put Mommy on and I'll ask her. You don't let me do anything."

The Box
(Life with Paola)

I live in a box.

The box has a lid. The lid has little holes in it. The holes let in air and a little light. The air and light make me want to do things. Some days, the desire to do things hits me like a wave. So I take the lid off the box and it becomes a boat. The box sails, propelled by the waves. They're not tidal waves, more like river currents. They start as sporadic ripples that soon become little whirlpools. The one that manages to suck me in first wins. It's almost never the whirlpool I initially expect. Inside the whirlpool, I put the lid back on the box. Air and light no longer come in through the holes, only water. The box never fills up all the way. When I reemerge from the whirlpool, I take the top off the box. The whirlpool has gotten me wet, but hasn't killed me.

I need the box to breathe. I need the holes in the lid to feed my desire. I need the waves to push me away. I need the whirlpools to go to the bottom of the river and realize the importance of the box. The box is the only way I have of doing things. In the silence of the box I dream of the beauty outside. In the beauty outside I miss the silence of the box.

Most people I've met have tried to pull me out of the box. Few people have come into the box with me. Those few didn't last long.

The person I live with now is the only one who ever brought her box inside mine.

To show me that it was actually the same.

Gianni

On the phone with Virginia:

"Daddy, I saw a snake in the woods with Grandpa today."

"What kind of snake, Virginia?"

"Grandpa said it was called a blind worm."

"A blind worm. That's okay then, it's not dangerous. Kisses, honey, now put your sister on the phone, would you?"

"Okay, Daddy. Bye!"

She passes the phone to Ginevra.

"Hi, Daddy! You know we-saw-a-GIANT-snake-with-Grandpa-today!"

"What do you know. What snake, Ginevra?"

"It's called Gianni."

Winning

Observing my daughters is a good way to establish certain things and put life into perspective.

For example, Paola is at the store right now, and we're playing, racing around the house.

I say, "One, two, three, go!" and they rocket off from the kitchen, go through the living room, down the hall, and into the bedroom. Then they race back the opposite way.

Virginia and Ginevra, the two older ones, are very serious about the race, elbowing and heckling each other, even accusing each other of cheating, because they truly care about coming in first. Sometimes one wins, sometimes the other.

Melania, on the other hand, runs after her sisters and is always behind. She often gets lapped, and the other two bump into her when they suddenly find her coming from the opposite way. But every time she gets back up and keeps going, laughing like crazy.

Melania doesn't care about winning. It's not even a competition for her; she doesn't even realize it's a race.

She just likes to run.

My Neighbor Has a Cow

My neighbor has a cow.

We're separated by a narrow strip of forest, and at this time of year, it's one big knot of plants, impenetrable to the eye. On the other side, there's a small stable, and above the stable, like Rapunzel's tower, sits my neighbor's house.

My neighbor's cow loves music. And my neighbor knows that happy cows make better milk. Therefore, around nine p.m. (or three on Sundays), my neighbor starts blasting a series of compilations. The woods resound with "Romagna mia, Romagna in fiore," "La mazurka del buon vino," "Volare," and other trendy hits.

When the cow is a little blue or has had a rough day, my neighbor puts the stereo on for her at night too. After dark, though, he keeps the volume low and changes the repertoire—like night and day, you could say. Then the woods whisper with Chopin and Haydn sonatas, but Beethoven remains the standard.

And there you are at one in the morning, your window open because of the heat, trying to be lulled to sleep by those moos that, mysteriously, are perfectly in tempo with the middle of the "Moonlight" piano sonata.

Then at some point, a wild boar shows up and it would be nice if Wagner started playing, but you can't have everything.

To Ourselves
(Mel & Me)

Melania and I have the house to ourselves till tomorrow.

Today, we spent the morning playing on the terrace,
first taking all the stuffed animals and blocks and
throwing them down on the lawn. Also on the terrace,
we spent an hour exercising as doctors recommend,
with her racing around on the scooter and me on the
skateboard, but we stopped after crashing into the
basil.

For lunch I made a rice salad. Melania managed to
eat only the rice, zigzagging around all the other ingredients and filling her little spoon one grain at a
time. When she finished her rice, she separated the
hot dog and tuna, gathered all the capers on one side
of the plate, and sorted everything else by color. She
made little towers with the cubes of cheese and
knocked them down by rolling baby onions and olives at them. Then she ate one thing at a time, except
for the capers, which she just sucked the salt off of
and spit them out like bugs that had flown into her

mouth. She wanted a roll, and then hollowed it out so much that by the time she was done with it, I could bring it to my ear and hear the sea. She stole the house phone twice. The first time I found it abandoned under the table, where it had been on the line with the pizza place for eighteen minutes. The second time she called the *Dylan Dog* cover artist. While I was in the bathroom, she stole a marker and drew a huge red *X* from her belly button to the top of her chest and now she looks like she's going in for gallbladder surgery. I put her down to sleep around two. She woke up half an hour ago, singing "Frère Jacques" and then shouting "Dormey-voo!" I opened the door and brought her up, she wanted an ice cream, and today she got the ice cream sandwich. One of the cookies wound up stuck to the TV screen, the other took off on an exploratory mission in the mop bucket, and we're waiting on probe photos like the ones of Pluto. She took the ice cream from the middle, rolled it over crumbs of crackers and chips from this morning, and managed to make a perfect cold dumpling, which she then happily ate, but only half. She insistently offered me the other half and I didn't want to offend her. Besides the faint aftertaste of marker, it wasn't half bad.

Now we're here, done with the *Peppa Pig* episode where George catches a cold, and we're trying to decide whether to call Grandma and Grandpa, call back the pizza place, or call my publisher and sing all of "Twinkle, Twinkle, Little Star" into the receiver. We'll see.

Face Stickers

As we were having breakfast this morning, Ginevra asked me a question.

"Daddy," she said, "why do people go to heaven when they die?"

Since she's been circling around the subject of death for a while now, and because the other day she interrogated her mother on the same topic, I played dumb in order to understand more clearly.

"How do you mean, Ginevra?" I asked.

"Why do we only go to heaven when we're dead? It would be much better to go there alive!"

"Well, Ginevra," I said, "it's because the living are too heavy."

"Why?"

"Because our body acts as ballast. Do you know what that is?"

"No," she said.

"It's a type of anchor, like the ones ships have," I said. "It keeps us here just like boats docked at port or boats that usually sail in shallow waters. When the anchor disappears, the boat goes out to sea forever."

"So we're like boats, Daddy?"

"In a certain sense."

"Then when we die it's like going to the sea?"

"Well," I said. "We're always at sea, even now. But perhaps when we die, we won't be afraid to go where the water is really high."

She paused for a long time.

"But Virginia told me that when you die you become see-through. I want to be see-through!"

"Ginevra, you'll only be like that to people who don't know you," I said. "When you die, the people who love you will see you anyway, even if you're see-through, you know?"

"How?"

"They see you in their memories," I said. "It's kind of like when you look out the window in the car. It's transparent, but since you put your stickers on it, you'll always be able to recognize it. So memories, for people, work pretty much the same way."

"What about when you're still alive?" she asked.

"What?"

"When you're still alive, you can't be see-through?"

"When you're alive, no," I said. "Even if sometimes, some days, it can happen that some people don't see you. It's as if you were invisible rather than transparent. It's like when it's dark out and you can't see any-thing."

"How come?"

"Because to really see other people, every day, you need to look carefully, so you can see even in the dark, even at night, like cats."

She thought about that for a moment.

"Daddy," she said. "I can see you at night, did you know that?"

"Me too, Ginevra," I said. "That's why I come to give you little kisses while you sleep."

"I know."

"You know?"

"Yeah, because kisses are like face stickers, right?"

"Yes, Ginevra," I said. "Exactly like that."

"And that's why we have to give lots of them," she said, "so we never become see-through."

Us Two

"Why do you love me?" she asked him once. He was chopping carrots.

He stopped and said, "Because I do."

"What do you mean because I do?" she said. "What kind of answer is that?"

He put the knife down and turned to her. "Why do you like Coke?" he asked her.

"What does that have to do with it?" she said.

"Answer me," he said.

"Because it's good," she said. "Because I like it, because it's Coke!"

"Well," he said, "I don't really like Coke, I prefer beer."

"I don't like beer," she said.

"That's why I love you," he said.

"Because I don't like beer?" she said.

"In a certain sense," he said.

She looked at him, he resumed chopping.

"What are the carrots for?" she asked.

"For the chicken curry," he said.

"I think chicken curry is gross," she said.

"I know," he said. "But tonight I felt like it, and so for you, I ordered a pizza."

"With olives?" she asked.

"Of course," he said.

"Did you get me a Coke too?" she said.

"Yes," he said.

"Give me a kiss," she said.

"Okay," he said, and he kissed her.

"You taste like beer," she said.

"I'm sorry," he said. "Hold on, I'll go brush my teeth."

And then she said, "Kiss me again."

The Typical Day of the
Comics Artist Father

It goes like this.

It's five-thirty in the morning. I go down to the studio. I browse through Facebook and have my coffee. I read the headlines in the *Repubblica*. Check my e-mail, you never know.

I sit at the table and turn on the light. The blank page stares at me. I stare back. We stay like that until one of us decides to look away—usually me.

I get up. I flip through something by Williamson or Boucq, just for a little inspiration. Instead it makes me depressed.

I look out the window. It's dawn and it's raining. I sit back down at the table. I start doodling randomly to loosen my hand. They're not really drawings, more like a jumble of shapes, blobs, pen pressure tests. Faces.

Only at that point do I open the script. I read the page. If there's dialogue, I read it out loud first, without lingering on the rest. If I can picture the scene, the expressions, without needing to go back to see where they are or why, then it's done. I skim the other information (setting, frames) and start to jot down a quick layout on regular paper. No reference points, not even the borders, nothing. Just to assess the hard parts.

At that point the real fun begins: I take the layout, scan it, print it on ledger paper. I google various references or inspiration on the work of the masters. Then I'm ready to start trying to define the whole thing on a larger page.

That's usually the moment when I hear a voice from the stairs.

"Daddyyy!"

Don't move. Maybe it was just your imagination.

"Daddyyyyyyyyy!!"

Stay put. It's an auditory hallucination.

"DADDYYYYYYYYYYYY!!!!"

Okay, it's not.

"Yes, Virginia?"

"Melania's awaaaake!"

"Ah. I'll be right up. And Ginevra?"

"She went to go pee-pee."

This around 7:40 or so.

I turn everything off, the panel looks at me longingly, "Take My Breath Away" starts playing in my head. I go upstairs. I give the oldest girl breakfast and prepare milk for the little one. I go to get the middle one. She's in the other room jumping on the bed next to a dead body. The body opens one bloodshot eye that shines in the dark and stares at me. Fortunately, I've studied eye language. It says, "Let me sleep at least one more hour, please. I went to bed at three." It must be said that in eye language "please" and "go drop dead" are damned similar.

I gather the girls and we go into the living room to watch cartoons. The middle one starts writing on the walls, the oldest tries to get kisses from the youngest who is just sticking her fingers in her eyes and giving her the hold Tatsumi Fujinami used to take down Riki Choshu in '83. I finish the leftovers of a chocolate Danish, pick up my iPad and start answering e-mails at random.

When Lazarus rises—within a time span that ranges from about an hour to next Wednesday—we split up the girls: the little one comes down to the studio with me, the older girls upstairs with her. Sometimes, vice versa.

Note that it's a Tuesday in August, any regular week. The whole summer has been like this.

In ten days, school starts again.

I want to cry.

Open Letter to Fedez

Dear Fedez,

We don't know each other, so first let me introduce myself: My name is Matteo Bussola, and I'm a father.

I'm writing you because the oldest of my three daughters, Virginia, at the age of eight and a half, has declared herself with preteen confidence "your greatest living fan" (I've tried to explain to her that singers don't have many zombies for fans, but . . .). Then I thought how there are people out there who even like acts like Berlusconi's crony Mariano Apicella, and so I started to think maybe she's right. I should also mention that Virginia is convinced that throughout your whole career you've only written three songs, which she listens to on repeat on her iPod (the others are excluded due to age), and thus, I think I can say she appreciates you for your music, and not because you're famous.

Virginia's biggest wish in the world is to get your autograph. Now, I am unashamed to admit, Fedez, I would have preferred my daughter to be a fan of Julio Iglesias like her dad, or even *Force Five: Grandizer*, but I know we don't choose our passions—they just happen—and so here we are. I had thought about sending you a message on Facebook, but I saw that it was impossible, then I thought of writing on your wall, but I imagined you'd never read such a long post even if it were Christmas, so in the end I thought, "Let's see if that story about six degrees of separation is true; if it's true everyone is on Facebook and things can happen." So I told myself maybe it was better to go about it that way; maybe someone in my contacts knows you and would be generous enough to pass along my message, who knows. Among other things, I forgot to tell you I'm a comic book illustrator for Sergio Bonelli Editore and my partner is a script writer for *Dylan Dog*, so if you're by chance a fan of comics—do you read *Dylan Dog* or *Tex* or *Zagor*?—for example, maybe I could do an original drawing of your favorite character for you, signed of course, in exchange for your autograph? What do you say? Also, consider that we're also a little bit famous in our field, nothing comparable to your level, of course, but let's say, if we were singers, my partner would be a superstar like Biagio Antonacci and I'd be a local favorite like Ivano e Gli Amici del Liscio. Sure, I know you're thinking, "Ivano who?" but I do my best and that's all I've got. I should also say I watch *X Factor* from time to time too, and when I saw you so touched by Lorenzo Fragola's audition the other day, I realized I shouldn't be afraid to write you. Most of all, when my daughter said to me, "Daddy, what can we do? I *have* to get Fedez's autograph!" with a look I've never seen from her before, not even the time she begged me to go with her on Oblivion at Gardaland—and I get the dizzies so bad I want to die—it was then I looked her in the eyes and said, "Virginia, let's try." But besides the fact that, as the great Yoda says, "Do or do not, there is no try," I'm reasonably certain that Virginia understood "try" to mean, "Don't worry. Daddy will handle it."

And so, dear Fedez, I ask you, don't make me look bad in front of her. Because a world where eight-year-old daughters lose the hope that their fathers can make their dreams come true, well that I think would be the worst world of all, perhaps you would agree.

I thank you in advance from the bottom of my heart, even if just for reading this.

Yo, *o bella frate'*, *o bagna càuda*, or you know, whatever you say.

Fedez-fully yours,

Matteo Bussola

FALL

Never Completely

I just took Melania to her first day of nursery school after the long summer break.

The cubby room was teeming with well-dressed parents holding infants, crammed together closer than mussels on sea rocks. There were so many people—I think some must have gotten there at five in the morning just to get in first. The parents all sort of had that look like, "This is the end!" or "This is the beginning!" or "I'm finally getting my life back!" Handing over the little ones was a wrenching series of crying fits. Melania and I were cry number seven. It didn't last long, but the high note à la Maria Callas at the end won us the critics' choice award.

When I left, I felt a little guilty before I even got to the bottom of the stairs. I got in the car, and there were no daughters in the back, just empty car seats. I wanted to stop by the newsstand, but I knew Paola was waiting anxiously at home, so I went back right away. I walked in, and there was Virginia lying on the couch watching *The Lord of the Rings* as Ginevra accosted me to ask if she could have the last chocolate egg. Paola was waiting for me in the bedroom, with that dreamy, slightly lost look that cormorants have when they're flying and their fish falls out of their beak.

"Well?" she said to me.

"It was fine," I said.

"Come on, tell me what happened!" she replied.

"Nothing," I said. "She went in like everything was okay, then she started wailing like she was never going to see me again."

Paola looked at me vacantly, like that fish wriggling in the flying cormorant's beak when it's still falling but hasn't hit the water yet, not knowing whether the fall will be its salvation or its end.

"Which teacher was it?" she asked.

"There were two," I said. "I'm going to make myself a coffee."

I left the room, and Virginia followed to ask for some warm milk. I asked her if she wanted sugar and prepared the milk for her. I took my coffee and went down to the studio.

Now here I am. I no longer hear shouting from upstairs, or the pitter-patter of tiny feet, or towers of blocks falling down. Part of me is happy because it knows that in the next few days, the time I have to work will seem to expand like a bubble. The other part suffers from road lag, that thing parents get when they suddenly realize the path ahead of them is free again, but they're a week behind in their heads, still writing one-handed with a head on their shoulder and cookie crumbs on their shirt.

It gets better day by day, but you never recover completely.

The Best Part
(*Les Enfants Qui S'aiment*)

In the city, on the way back from the mechanic, I'm in traffic waiting for the light to turn. It's a bright sunny day, it's almost one, we're on the bridge, and the air is too warm for September. All the cars have their windows down.

Right beside me in the next lane, there's a white Twingo. Inside there's a boy at the wheel and a girl with long, straight brown hair, both twenty or so. They start making out. They kiss and I watch them as I would admire a sunset, or sunrise, or mountain waterfall. I almost feel like an old peeping tom, but I can't pry myself away. The kisses are long, exhaustive, fiery. They take short breaks in which the girl puts her head on the boy's shoulder and he strokes her hair. Then she grabs his head, almost forcefully, and they start up again. They're beautiful. I watch them and think back to when that's what things used to be like, or better yet when that was the only thing, when it was all kissing and no problems, no money, no mortgage, work somewhere in the future. When responsibility, essentially, was still just a word. When the only important thing was living, nothing else.

At some point a car honks close by. The girl detaches from the boy, almost startled, the boy turns around. The honking came from the guy in the Audi behind them. The light had turned green maybe half a second ago—we can't even go yet, but he honked. And I think, what kind of person honks at a couple of kids kissing. I almost want to get out of my car, as if it were a personal affront. "Where do you have to go, asshole?" I think. "Now I'm not going to move until you pass by so I can get a look at your face."

Then my lane starts moving and the guy behind me starts honking too. I make a gesture at him that's halfway between "sorry" and "go fuck yourself," and start moving. I see the Twingo with the two young people a few car lengths ahead, with their left turn signal on. When we're beside each other again the girl looks out the window and our eyes meet for a moment. In that moment, she's smiling. The smile isn't for me but that doesn't matter. It's the best part of my day today.

When I get back home, Virginia has just returned from school. I find her at the gate with her backpack still on. I get out of the car and open the gate for her. For a moment, I imagine her as a twenty-year-old, and sadly it's not even that hard to do.

"Daddy," she says, "what are we eating today?"

"Virginia," I say, "I just got back myself. How about spaghetti with tuna and olives?"

"Okay, sounds good!" she says.

I see her smile as she runs into the house, and I'm suddenly assailed by a twinge of guilt about the girl in the Twingo.

Because the best part of my day has been replaced by another.

Mobile Dining

The phone rings. There's no number. I don't answer. The phone rings again. There's no number. I don't answer.

A few minutes go by. The phone rings again. The number is from Milan. I'm tempted not to answer, but since I don't know all the Bonelli phone numbers by heart it's better not to risk it. It could be one of the editors.

"Hello?"

"Hello, good morning. May I speak to the member of the household who does the shopping?"

"The shopping? Sorry, what shopping are you talking about?"

"The shopping."

"Shopping like the supermarket, farmers' market, et cetera?"

"Exactly."

"That's me."

"Ah. Good morning, ma'am."

"I'm a man."

"Oh, sorry, I hope I didn't offend you."

"I'm not offended. Shall we get to the point?"

"Yes, of course. Mister . . . Bussola, right?"

"Yes, go ahead."

"We're a new grocery delivery company, a new shopping service."

"Mmh."

"We're reaching out to potential customers to let them know about our grocery delivery services. May I tell you about them?"

"Grocery wha?"

"Home shopping."

"You mean, you'd like to help me take my groceries home? Like for little old ladies?"

"Not quite, Mr. Bussola. It's not that we help you with them, we deliver them directly to your home."

"I see. No thank you."

"Why not? You'll find it's very practical, think about it: you're working, you don't know what to make for dinner, there's nothing in the fridge. You call us or go to our Web site, it only takes a second to register, and you can do your shopping from the office or wherever you like, with a choice of the best products on the market. We deliver the groceries to your home at whatever time you request."

"Well, listen, besides the fact that I don't have an office—"

"It was just an example; you can also do it from your smartphone."

"I don't have a smartpho—"

"Then you can call us from your landline."

"Will you let me finish?"

"Sorry."

"I was saying, besides no office or smartphone, I enjoy going to the grocery store too much. It's one of the pleasures of my life, not to mention one of the rare occasions when I get out of the house. I would never delegate it to someone else."

"I see. May I ask why?"

"Why what?"

"Why you never leave the house?"

"Are you butting into my personal business?"

"No, no, excuse me, I didn't mean to pry."

"During the day I work, that's it. After three, my daughters are home from school."

"I don't see the problem."

"When they get back they dress me up."

"They dress you up?"

"As a prince."

"Oh."

"Sometimes I play Adelino."

"Adelino?"

"Adelino kidnaps princesses."

". . ."

"And I can't go out dressed like a prince, or Adelino. I mean, I've tried, but . . . you know."

"Sorry, but didn't you say you go out to do the shopping?"

"What difference does that make? That's a matter of survival. And besides, I like it too much."

"But you go dressed as a prince?"

"Not always. Last time I was dressed as Dame Gothel."

"Dame Gothel?"

"Rapunzel's mother."

"Good day, sir."

Light

In the car, on the way to nursery school:

"Daddy, look! Three Eiffel Towers!"

"Those aren't Eiffel Towers, Ginevra. They're electricity towers."

"No, they're Eiffel Towers!"

"No, Ginevra. They look like that. But there's only one real Eiffel Tower and it's in a place called Paris."

"That's where Lollo lives."

"No. Lollo lives in Arbizzano. But you're right, where he lives, there's a big electricity tower. But they're not really towers—they're structures that hold power lines. Like for light."

"Light?"

"Yes, light. When you turn on the lamp in your room at home, the light comes from those wires there."

She looks out in the direction of the towers.

"There it is, Daddy!"

"What?"

"The light!"

"No, Ginevra, you can't see the light inside the wires."

"But I saw it go by!"

"Oh yeah? And where was it going?"

"To my room, because it doesn't know I'm going to nursery school right now."

"Don't worry, when I get home I'll let it know."

"Yes. Tell it before you go down to your studio—that way you'll be able to see."

"Okay."

"But tell it to come back upstairs at night because Mommy has to read me stories."

"I'll tell it, I'll tell it."

"Also, Daddy?"

"Yes?"

"How come you can talk to the light?"

"Hmm. Because when I was little I was really afraid of the dark, but Grandma and Grandpa didn't want to keep the lights on at night. And so I learned to summon it."

"How?"

"I would close my eyes really tight and curl up under the covers and then think about something I liked. That way I wasn't afraid anymore and the light came."

"Did it come from the wires?"

"Well . . . some from the wires, some from my thoughts."

"Thoughts can make light, Daddy?"

"Yeah, they can make a lot. Kids' thoughts especially."

"So can the Eiffel towers, though."

"That's true."

We arrive at the nursery school. We sit on the bench in front of the cubbies. I put her smock on.

"Daddy, do kids' thoughts, the ones that make light, have buttons to press like the lamp by my bed?"

"Well, Ginevra, not all of them do. But some do, yes."

"And where is it?"

I look at her sideways and she stares at me knowingly because she has figured out what comes next.

"Here!" I say, pushing on her side, where I know she's ticklish.

She bursts out laughing so loud I can't imagine what she's thinking about, but it must be a wonderful thought, because it makes such a bright, warm light that it would put even Paris to shame.

Prejudice

hear the dogs barking, I know that someone's about to push the buzzer at the front gate. It rings. I'm chopping onions and right in the middle of making sauce, but since Paola is giving Melania a bath, she wins, and I have to go. The intercom has been broken for a while now, so as usual I push aside the curtain to look out. There's a young black man with a duffel bag on his back. I think about not letting him in. I'm afraid the sauce will start sticking to the saucepan. And all I'd say to him anyway is, "No thanks, I don't need anything" and then end up buying a packet of tissues for five euros as usual anyway. I get over my laziness because I figure I should at least answer the bell. Before going out I make sure I have at least five euros in my pocket. I go outside and walk up to the gate. He's smiling, says hello, I say hello back. I wait for him to pull the duffel bag off his back.

Instead he says, "Excuse me, could you please give me some water?" and he holds out an empty plastic bottle.

I feel like a shithead. "Of course," I say. I take the bottle, go inside, fill it up, grab a bottle of sparkling water from the fridge. I come back out and hand him both. He doesn't seem to understand.

"Take this one too," I tell him. "It's colder." He smiles, surprised, and thanks me. We say goodbye and he goes off.

When I get back inside the sauce isn't even sticking a little.

The News Vendor

"So, Mr. Matteo, anything new coming out?"

The news vendor always does this; he asks me every time now. I rue the day that, in order to convince him to put up a flyer, I let slip the phrase, "I did that comic."

"What do you mean, did it?"

"I did it."

"In what sense, did it? Drew it? How do you manage to draw so small?"

And from there followed the inevitable catalogue of niceties: "Huh, do you get paid for it?" "Oh, you draw them by hand?" "So, do you write the bubbles or draw the pictures first?"

For once and for all, the bubbles, or rather, the balloons, are not the text. The dialogue is written first and is only put inside the balloons at the end, et cetera.

At any rate, after giving him advance notice about the release of *Lukas* and *Orfani* in the last few months—more than anything to stop him from displaying them next to *Poochie*—and alerting him about all the Cosmo releases (so he'd hold them for me), yesterday I finally informed him of the upcoming debut of *Adam Wild*, the new Bonelli comic set in Africa, about which I could boast of being one of the illustrators.

Today I stop by.

"There he is!" I hear before I'm even through the door. "Mr. Matteo, there's someone here who reads *Zagor*," the news vendor says merrily. He announces this as if it were an event.

"Oh," I say. "Great."

I shoot a glance at the guy. He's around fifty, well dressed, hefty. He has hands like Gianni Morandi's.

"What do you do?" the *Zagor* guy says, point blank.

Caught by surprise, I don't understand right away. "What?" I ask.

"For *Zagor*," he asks.

"Oh, no, no. I don't draw *Zagor*. I'm working on a series called *Adam Wild*," I say.

"Oh yeah, I saw the ad!" he says. "The one about Africa!"

"That's the one," I say.

"And which issue are you drawing in the Africa series?" he says.

"Well, I'm working on two at the same time. I'm inking number eleven and drawing all of number twenty," I say.

He stares at me. He has the expression of someone who's just had a realization. I do too—I realize I'm going to be subjected to his.

"But the first issue hasn't come out yet," he says. "You can't be drawing number twenty! Or do you already know everything that's going to happen *after*?"

I try to remain calm.

"Eh eh eh, he knows everything *before*," the proud news vendor intervenes.

"In fact the issues are written and drawn well ahead of time," I explain. "The first twenty-four issues of *Adam* are already being produced, for example. But that's the norm," I say. "That's how it works with *Zagor* also."

"What do you mean?" he says.

"I mean that the artists who work on *Zagor* draw their issues even years before they hit the shelves."

"*Years*, really?" he says.

"Years," I confirm.

"Even the ones who do the covers?" he says.

"Even them," I say.

"You see? I told you this guy knows *everything*!" the news vendor says, piling it on. "So now, when's this issue of *Zagor* coming out, Mr. Matteo?"

I look at them both and for a second I feel like I'm in the middle of Kansas in a Wes Craven film. The best part is I *know* exactly what's about to happen.

"Would you draw me something?" the guy asks. Just like that. Like it's nothing. At eight in the morning. Like I have "insert coin" written on my forehead, but obviously, without any mention of a coin.

"Um, you know, I'm double parked, and I don't even have a pen." I pretend not to see the news vendor stretching a hand toward the pack of new Bics behind him. "And I'm taking the girls to school. But tell you what, I'll draw you something at home, then tomorrow or the day after I'll bring it to you here, okay? If I don't see you I'll leave it with him," I say, indicating the news vendor, who's holding twenty-four Bics in his fist.

"Ah, that would be great, thanks!" he says.

"What do you want in the drawing?" I ask, to avoid any misunderstandings.

He looks at me as if I'd just sworn in church.

"Zagor!" he says.

"Yeeeah. But I don't draw *Zagor*," I go.

They both stare at me with glassy, incredulous eyes like green lizards.

"Okay, Zagor then," I say.

"Zagor in Africa," he goes.

I think, "How 'bout a pound of flesh too, while we're at it?" But I don't say it.

"Zagor in Africa, okay," I say. "See you later then, bye."

I leave.

"Mr. Matteo!" the voice reaches me as I'm opening the car door.

"What?" I say.

"Will you draw me something too?" says the news vendor.

"Huh?" I say.

"A drawing," he says.

"Not for tomorrow, though." I want to make that clear right away.

"No, no," he goes. "Don't worry. By Saturday is fine."

I feel a certain Venetian swear word rise up inside me. On the outside, however, I almost smile, incredulous.

"What do you want?" I say to him, already prepared for the worst.

"Canon," he tells me.

"Canon?" I repeat.

"Yeah, Canon. The warrior. The barbarian," he specifies as if to say, "Don't you know anything?"

"Canon," I repeat again, trying to fight back the tears. "Perfect."

"In Africa," he adds.

"Canon the barbarian, in Africa," I say. "Okay, bye then."

"Bye!" he says.

At this point I see only two possible paths ahead of me:

1. I switch newsstands, vanishing into obscurity forever like a ninja.
2. I go on Saturday and bring him a drawing of a photocopier in the savannah with a leopard on top.

Letter to My Daughter
Who Is Growing Up

Dear Virginia,

   I'm writing you because there are mornings
when I see you clearly, while you're getting
ready for school, and this is one of them. With
your red beret that frames your sparkling eyes
and your backpack that's always too heavy
and your snack that's almost never the one you
want, you're so adorable I want to just hug you
and never let go.
   You endure the thankless role of being the
oldest, and unfortunately not much can be
done about it. You always have to be the best,
you're the only one who cleans up after
herself, you're the one who has to see her toys
snatched by her younger sisters, and you often
have to keep quiet. It was the same for me too,
you know. And I know middle children think
the same thing and the youngest too—
everyone has their struggles. Let's just say

this: having shared your fate of being the oldest, I understand your situation best.

I'd like to tell you that you're the origin of everything. That, if it weren't for you, your mother and I might have split up, crushed by the wall of our differences. Instead, you gave us a way to see opportunities in those differences. Thus, even if you don't know it, you're responsible for everything that came afterward: your two sisters, this house, the strength I have today and owe most of all to you. Which is another way of saying that your mother and I owe it to ourselves, but you are still the best synthesis.

You're very pretty. By now it's clear that this will be a big problem. For me, too. Because I know beauty doesn't protect you from anything. Not from people's superficiality, not from pain, not from difficulties or defeats. Standing by and seeing these things come along, separately or all at once, will be incredibly hard. Many think of beauty as a sort of umbrella. But sometimes it's a bag where you can't breathe. I hope it's not like that for you, but if it ever is, know that I'll be there with you to poke all the air holes you need.

You also have the misfortune of being very

intelligent and have inherited the empathetic sensibility of you-know-who. And that is what will make you suffer most.

I promise you from now on that if you want to make comics you'll make comics, and if you want to play the harp you'll play the harp, and neither your mother nor I will ever try to push you toward something just because it resembles us. You will always do only what you want. In return, you have to do your best. Teaching you this lesson is one of my main duties as your parent.

I'm writing you because I'm not embarrassed to do so, just as I'm not embarrassed about my feelings, but most importantly because this letter will last. And since everything will be digital when you grow up—maybe even love—it might be easier to leave you these words between the pages of an old book, written in twelve-point Garamond just for you.

I think you know the rest, so I won't write it.

Nonetheless, I'll make sure that you feel it, every day.

The Kiss

go to pick up Melania from nursery school.

She starts smiling the moment she sees me and runs over to me as if I'd come out of nowhere to save her. Her surprise is due to the fact that I usually take her in the morning while Mommy usually picks her up in the afternoon.

We get her jacket out of her cubby, put on her shoes, put her slipper socks back, and go out. At the bottom of the stairs, there's a little blond boy crying inconsolably. He's a little younger than her, about eighteen months old—Melania could be his caretaker. The boy's mother looks at him as if she wants to pick him up, but she has another child in one arm and is holding on to a stroller with the other. Melania goes over to the boy and stands in front of him. She gives him a hug, and then a soft kiss on the cheek. The boy stops crying almost immediately, as if someone has flicked a switch. The mom and I look at each other. My uncertain look says "sorry," because Melania has a bit of a cold and you never know how moms will take these things, but her expression seems inclined toward "thank you."

"See how nice the little girl is, Denis?" the mom says. "Why don't you give her a kiss too?"

The boy looks at my daughter; my daughter looks at him. Denis hops forward, grabs her head, throws his mouth wide open like a shark, and straight up Frenches her. Surprised, Melania takes offense and pushes him away. He falls on his little behind and starts crying even louder than before.

The mom shoots me a look that says, "What's with your daughter—first she acts easy and then she changes her tune!"

My look, on the other hand, says, "If we give you a lip, it doesn't mean you can take the tongue."

Melania shows me that she wants to be picked up. We say goodbye and walk away, while Denis watches her like a cat does a bird just escaped from its cage.

When we're in the car, buckling her into her car seat, I say, "Melania, you need to stop this kissing thing."

She stares at me with a serious look, then she starts to laugh. Finally she licks me across the face from my chin all the way up to my forehead. I close the door, laughing myself, and wipe the slobber off with the sleeve of my sweatshirt. I turn just in time to catch the hateful glare of the blond boy peeking out from behind his mother's back. He has an unmistakable look that says, "Go ahead and laugh, you old bastard. Give me thirteen years or so and I'll be the one laughing."

On the way home, Melania sings her "Frère Jacques" made up entirely of vowels.

I have "Highway to Hell" on a loop in my head, and I remember that the other day in the hardware store, I saw packs of barbed wire on sale.

The Coat

I was sick last night and had a dream that left me with a thick residue of fear. A few hours of intermittent sleep don't exactly foster warm feelings about getting up, but I knew that forcing myself to lie there would have been useless.

I tried going down to the studio early and working, because putting my hand on the page is the best therapy for clearing my thoughts. It didn't work. I went back upstairs at seven, made breakfast for everyone, and woke the girls up for school. Ginevra had a cold and I decided to keep her home. Paola did their hair and laid out their clothes, then went back to sleep since she'd gone to bed very late. I had another coffee, the fear was still there, and something was going on with Ginevra.

"What's wrong, Ginevra?" I said.

"I'm mad at you," she said.

"And why's that?"

"Because you opened my pastry when I wanted to open it myself!"

"I'm sorry," I said. "You're right, tomorrow I'll give it to you and you can do it all by yourself."

"But you always do that! First you do something wrong and then you say sorry!"

The statement struck me because it's something her mother often says to me as well. When Paola and I fight—I'm almost always wrong, I admit—and I apologize, she says, "The door has already slammed in my face anyway."

It's true. If she's already gotten the door, apologies don't make much difference, that's how you should learn to pay attention. I worked for years to learn how to apologize, so I always think that my sincerity will be recognized and can make up for the damage. It almost never works that way.

I gave Ginevra a little kiss on the head and went to take Melania to school.

When we got there, we found a little boy by the cubbies. They played hide-and-seek and then ran into class. Then I went down to the nursery school to return a book Ginevra had borrowed. Going out into the yard without saying goodbye to her, without jumping in front of the window and seeing her laugh, gave me a strange feeling, as if I'd been robbed.

I went back to the car, and in the yard of the house across the way, there was a very old woman feeding some cats, six or seven of them. The woman was in a nightgown and slippers and had on a wool hat that was too small for her head. A young man who seemed about twenty came out from inside carrying a tan coat, which he gently placed over her shoulders. The woman didn't stop feeding the cats, nor did the man try to take her inside. They just stayed there finishing the job. The boy was bent over her, enveloping her with the coat, as if she were a little girl.

I stayed there watching them for almost a minute. In that time, observing them from a few yards away, it was as if that image were compensation for something.

When I got back in the car, the fear was no longer there.

Canon

Because unfortunately I'm unable to cure myself of being a man of my word, today I'm taking a drawing to the news vendor.

When he sees me, his face lights up like a lamp.

"Mr. Matteo!" he says. "*DY-lan Dog* is out and so is *Ken Parker* and even *BurBEHrry!*"

That last one must be a really hard-core Texas Ranger, I think.

"Yes," I say. "I know. I came by just to bring you your drawing."

"Oh, of course, of course," he says. "Thank-ee, sir."

I hand it to him. He opens it. On the page stands a magnificent "Canon" the Barbarian in Africa. Since nobody was paying me and I had no time and especially in light of the . . . um, comics savvy of the recipient, I basically copied a Buscema Conan without a shred of guilt. I even wrote a dedication: "Canon, for Renato, in friendship," because I didn't want to upset his convictions.

He stares at the picture, puzzled. He looks like someone trying to read Ikea instructions in Swedish.

"Is something wrong?" I ask.

"No, no," he says. "The drawing is wonderful. It's just that the name isn't right."

Here we go, I think, he's finally realized that the name is Conan, not Canon. That'll be a lesson not to give people any credit.

"My name is Rinaldo," he says, "not Renato."

The Visit

Today my mom is coming to visit.

When my mom comes over, even just for coffee, panic is unleashed throughout the house—the alert rises to Defcon 2, or even 1, depending on how much advance notice she gives us. For example, if I have three days' notice, I'll scrub and shine the stovetop, but if I have less than three hours' warning, I'll throw the burners straight into a vat of hydrochloric acid and polish them with carpenter-grade steel wool while wearing cast iron gloves. Then there's the pile of clothes that need ironing, which I affectionately call "Rodney" since it has made a permanent home on the living room couch for three years like a drunk Rodney Dangerfield sprawled across the hood of a Fiat Panda. Every time my mom visits, we roll it into the storage closet after checking to make sure a daughter hasn't accidentally wound up inside, or that half of a ham and mushroom sandwich that had disappeared followed by a week of accusations along the lines of "you ate it!" "no, you!" but had actually ended up in the pocket of my freshly laundered cardigan. I do a quick sweep of the bathroom; leave Garrett and Cordelia in the basement because my mom is afraid of them; and try with meticulous care to clear a path through the front yard that safely leads to the front door and is free of leaves or turds or pinecones, or turds that look like pinecones. But every time my mom forgets something in the car and has to go back, she accidentally takes the other path, the one with wild boars lurking in the tall grass like Viet Cong.

Anyway, every time my mom visits, I reflect on how it's usually with the people we love most that we try to hide who we really are, how we actually live. Because, age and distance and parenthood notwithstanding, we're always children too—we never manage to fully free ourselves of it. The fact is that as a child, and even as an adult, you're constantly afraid of disappointing, while as a parent, your role is to guide and protect.

And then I think about how even when we become parents, we're terrified of disappointing our children, every day, and we live pressed like a slice of cheese between two pieces of existential bread, between one source of guilt and another. And I think how nice it would be if, rather than being pressed by guilt, we could feel surrounded by beauty. That would mean seeing the beauty at the heart of things and showing it to others at the same time, without attributing it to what we're able or unable to do. Because our beauty isn't hidden by piles of wrinkled clothes or pinecones in the yard, but by everything we do to pretend that the pile of clothes and those pinecones aren't part of us, with our complications, the risks we choose to take, the decision to prioritize life over always trying to seem perfect. Those pinecones in the yard and that pile of wrinkled clothes and that dirty stove, in the end, say much more about us than everything else. They don't say we're bad people, or irresponsible, but that we go on in spite of everything, every day. And that just might be something to be proud of.

Today my mom is coming to visit.

I'll go to meet her at the gate, I'll bring her inside and make her a coffee on my dirty stove. I'll have her sit on the couch, on top of one of my wrinkled sweaters, the softest. I'll endure her look of thinly veiled disapproval with a smile, able to see the beauty behind it that only I, as a son, know so well.

That will be all we need.

Three Hundred and Forty-seven

Yesterday, I was talking to a friend of mine about how love, in the end, is always a distance to cross.

When it's short you can build a bridge across it. When it's long, at least one of the two will have to walk a ways. Because in a relationship there's always one who shifts more than the other, one who is more willing to come out of himself to be vulnerable and venture into the unknown and slippery territory of meeting in the middle. That's the reason why everyone, sooner or later in life, ends up becoming someone else's regret. It happens when the person who misses you realizes too late that she didn't accept the challenge of traveling her little part of the road. The best loves are the ones where you move together, starting from a great distance, sometimes only faintly sensing each other. Sniffing across miles or years apart. And then suddenly you meet right in the middle, as if that's where you were the whole time, at a point where one plus one doesn't necessarily make two, but can also make three hundred and forty-seven. Because love is never a perfect algebraic sum; it works more like throwing a stone in the water. When you meet someone you like, you make your move and stay there, counting the ripples that form. There are imperturbable personalities that don't ripple but stay smooth; others that make slow, wide circles; and still others that, in a mysterious way, begin to resonate with yours. You realize that it's because the waves are irregular; they come at unpredictable intervals, and when you think the inertia has died down, they start back up again. In that case, the ripples don't just flow across the water's surface; it's as if they originate from down below. Which shows that in the end, love is indeed a distance, but it comes from the depths, from something that must rise to the surface first. It's a sort of image that appears little by little, like a photograph being developed in a darkroom. Only a few people are capable of revealing that image, even to themselves. Why some and not others remains the real question.

The real answer is three hundred and forty-seven, or in other words, love.

Ears

I n the car, on the way to nursery school:

"Daddy, why do we have ears?"

"To hear with, Ginevra."

"No, but why do we *have* ears?"

"Because that way we can listen to words."

"No, but *why* do we have ea—"

"Because that way, when babies cry, mommies and daddies can hear them."

I look at her in the rearview mirror. She's gazing out the window, her expression serious.

"Daddy."

"Yes?"

"Mommies and daddies can hear when they laugh too, though."

I smile, thinking how much better her version is than mine.

"Yes, especially that."

When we're in the car and my daughter explains life to me, I always understand things better.

That's the reason I have ears, I'm sure.

Children's Dreams

go out to buy a large envelope in order to mail a drawing.

The stationery store is closed, so I go to the one down the street. At the counter, the clerk is talking to a lady who looks like Virna Lisi in *Time for Loving*.

"Bah, that's how they are at that age," the clerk says.

"Yeah, but at least have some real ambitions, come on," Virna Lisi says.

"Excuse me, do you by any chance have one of those big envelopes—the yellow padded ones?" I interrupt.

"Back there, go ahead and choose the size," says the clerk.

I go and start digging through the envelopes.

"Because," Virna Lisi says, "he thinks he's going to become Milo Manara one day. Do you know how many people in that line of work live hand to mouth?"

"Ah, mine's the same. When he was eleven he wanted to be an actor. After that he started a rock band and was a singer. Later I bugged him to get over it, he was convinced, and now that he has a little bub of his own, he works here with me."

"Exactly," Virna Lisi says. "These days you need to have your feet on the ground, at least a little, come on. Thank goodness my husband laid down the law and now he's decided to go to a science high school—that's a step in the right direction."

Hearing "science high school" I'm hit with déjà vu. I'm back in 1985, in my family's living room, Righeira is singing "L'estate sta finendo" and my father has just explained to me why I'm not going to art high school. I find the envelope I need and go to pay. Virna Lisi moves out of the way and pulls a sea green smartphone from her purse.

"So, how's it going?" the clerk asks me.

"Good, thank you," I answer, taken by surprise.

"Hey, you would know," she says. "Could you ask your bosses why the traffic light out here always quits working?"

"Well, ma'am, I haven't worked in public administration for a long time."

"Sure, I heard that," she says. "But you must still know everyone."

"I'll see what I can do," I say, cutting her short.

"So what are you up to now?" she says, shoving the envelope into a bag that's too small.

"What do you mean?" I say.

"For work," she says.

I think for a second before answering. I look over at Virna Lisi punching the buttons on her smartphone.

"I'm an actor in musicals," I say.

"You don't say," the clerk says. "Seriously?"

Virna Lisi looks up from her smartphone.

"Where do you act?" the clerk asks.

"Ah, wherever they hire me," I say. "Mostly at people's homes."

"People's homes?" she says.

"Yes," I say.

"Come on now," Virna Lisi says. "How do you act in people's homes? Going door to door? What do you do? I mean, what shows do you do?"

"Well," I say, "to be completely precise, I tell people to fuck off."

"To . . . what?" she says.

"To fuck off," I say. "But in their own home, eh! That's the hard part."

"But, what . . . ?" Virna Lisi says.

"Basically," I say, "I'm contacted by people who maybe have a problem with someone, or harbor an old grudge. They give me the recipient's address and I show up dressed as John Wayne, or Superman, or Rapunzel, sometimes even in regular clothes. Then I put a stereo on a little stand, and sing to them to go fuck themselves."

"Come on," Virna says, laughing. "That can't be real. What kind of job is that? Are there seriously people who hire you for that?"

"If only you knew," I say. "Rejected girlfriends. Ex-husbands. Political opponents. People who lost their job. But the ones who request me the most are children of overbearing parents, most of the time when they're already adults."

"Children?" she says.

"Yeah," I say. "By the way, do you happen to have a stereo here?"

"Uh, no," says the clerk.

"Never mind," I say. "I can sing a cappella."

Why the World Exists

Virginia and I are in the kitchen having breakfast.

"Daddy, why does the world exist?"

"Huh?"

"Why was space created?"

"What do you mean?"

"Couldn't it all have just been blank with a great big cockroach wandering around?"

"Egads, Virginia. I don't know. Truth is, maybe it would have been better that way."

"How come?"

"Because we've done so many bad things to our world. Cockroaches, however, haven't done anything."

"So then is the world mad at us?"

"Maybe not mad mad, but it's definitely not too happy with us."

"Can't we tell it we're sorry?"

"Every so often some people try, but there are never enough of them. And most people don't know how."

"Why not?"

"Because to say sorry you have to admit you did

something wrong, Virginia. And also because people tend to forget the most important part when they apologize. There was once a man named Randy Pausch who said that good apologies have three parts: I'm sorry, it was my fault, and how do I make it right. Well, almost everyone forgets the third part."

"Even with the world?"

"Especially with the world."

We put on our coats and I walk her out to catch the school bus. She looks thoughtful, vaguely sad.

"Daddy."

"Yeah?"

"I lost my technology binder."

"Oh, Virginia. You're telling me this now? Did you need it today?"

"Yeah."

"Okay, listen. The first thing you should do when you get to class is tell the teacher. This morning you can do your technology assignments on a piece of paper, and then we'll put it in a new binder."

"I'm sorry, Daddy. It's my fault."

"And what else?"

"And I can't find my pencil sharpener either."

Lucca Comics

Early tomorrow morning—so we say (we hope to leave early every time, but then can't manage to get away before eleven)—Paola and I are going to start making our way to the Lucca Comics convention.

I say "start" because the trip includes various stops. Aside from waking, dressing, feeding, shaving, locking the windows, throwing our luggage in the car, changing Melania's diaper again, turning off the gas, waiting for the guy from the dog hotel, "do I bring the book or not," "can't find my glasses," "who the hell opened the crackers that were for the trip," "lost my toothbrush," etc., we have to make the following stops:

- Stop one at our oldest daughter's school to pick up the books that Virginia carelessly left on her desk but needs for her homework while we're there.

- Stop two at the gas station to check tires/water/oil, "Look how cute those tropical mango air fresheners are," "Daddy I have to go pee-pee."

- Stop three at Grandma and Grandpa Bussola's to drop off Ginevra. You live through your mother's coffee and your father's "How's work going?" as well as your middle daughter's elaborate, heartbreaking goodbye.

- Stop four at Grandma and Grandpa Barbato's lake house to drop off the screaming baby and the oldest daughter, who is supposed to act as a deterrent to her younger sister's screams. You live through Paola's father's coffee, Virginia's hugs that on these occasions always remind you of the little match girl with her last match fighting the wind on Christmas night, peel Melania off your legs, and leave a valley of tears behind you. Turn back because "Oh no, we left their hats in the car."

- Stop five at Paola's favorite roadside stop. We always miss it because every time it's "the next one," and then we can never figure out why we end up eating the same soggy sandwich at that café/shack in the middle of the A15.

- Stop six on the A15, where invariably, right after our sandwiches, I say, "All right then, the worst is over, the rest will be a breeze." But at the *B* in "breeze," we catch sight of the dozens of miles of traffic backed up between us and Viareggio.

• Stop seven in La Spezia because "I told you to turn left."

We reach Lucca at around six p.m., if all goes well. I arrange my suits elegantly in the closet; Paola unpacks her suitcase, making the usual pile of stuff right in the middle of the bed. We get the first phone call from Grandma and Grandpa Barbato who pretend everything is fine. Shortly afterward comes the second, during which it becomes clear that they're in a state of panic.

At that point, two paths appear before us, one of which is, "What do you say, it's almost seven, should we go check out the convention for a bit?"

But I choose the less traveled: delivery pizza out of the box in the hotel room, reruns of *Embarrassing Bodies* or *Rocky* on YouTube, and bed at ten, because these are the only and I mean the *only* three nights in the entire year when I'll be able to sleep uninterrupted until eight in the morning without daughters waking me up or dogs barking at boars or people calling at 7:05 because my number is just like the pediatrician's office's except for the last digit.

At 10:15 my mother usually calls to ask if we got there all right.

New Shoes

For two weeks she's been asking what I want for my birthday.

For two weeks I've been putting off the answer, trying to drag it out.

How can I tell her that, well, I need a new computer, but we can't afford it, so really it isn't even necessary; that I'd like these Japanese pens I saw on a Web site but I always color with the first thing I grab anyway and I have fun that way; that if we could, I'd like to get a cleaning lady to come once a week; or that maybe I'd like a tablet that allows me to click on a link and open it before the fifth try and that doesn't crash whenever I hit send?

That a crate of craft beer would be nice, or a Neal Adams drawing, or maybe just a few pairs of socks without holes in them. Even a pair of new shoes, maybe. Or maybe a more robust constitution, though maybe I'd better ask Santa Claus for that.

Basically, how can I tell her that I'd like a bunch of things but don't really need anything? Because everything I need, everything that gives my life meaning, every motivation, she's already given me—to the point that the best birthday gift I can even imagine would be a long, passionate kiss by the window while it's raining outside and I have her head in my hands?

Maybe I'll just not tell her and hope.

Although, some new shoes . . .

To keep walking together down this long road, I'll need them.

Boy Hair

I n the car, on the way to nursery school:

"Daddy, why did you get a haircut?"

"Because it was getting too long, Ginevra. And I promised Grandma."

"Ugh."

"What, you don't like it?"

"No."

"Oh, no, why not?"

"Because before you just looked like a dad, but now you look like a boy!"

Taking Care

I went to the newsstand early this morning.

Rinaldo had set aside a comic for me, and since it was a clear day and the air was good and I had parked far away, on my way back to the car I decided to sit in the playground for a few minutes and leaf through my new purchase.

There were only three of us at the playground. Maybe because it wasn't even nine yet and a little chilly out. Across from my bench there was a sleepy-looking man in his forties pushing a little girl on the swings, probably his daughter. The little girl seemed around four, had long messy hair, and was wearing a purple jacket and a scarf that were both too big for her. I thought of Ginevra, of how I used to push her on the swings, and of how now she does it all by herself and tells me not to touch her. Of Virginia, who's no longer interested in swings and just wants to climb trees. Of Melania, who has just discovered them and every time she sees one can't be made to get off; she even wants to go on the big-kid ones and has just figured out how to swing back and forth with her legs, which if you see her try, you can't help but laugh.

At a certain point, the man pushed a bit too hard and the girl fell forward into the grass. He got her right away, before she could even get scared, almost before she even realized she'd fallen. Before she started to cry. He pulled her up and crouched down in the grass, and the little girl hugged him; and they stayed like that for a while, his hand on her head, her head buried in his chest. Completely still. I watched them and I knew well the guilt that was visible on the man's face, the fear of not being there even for one crucial moment—I feel it every day. But I also knew that for the girl, being held tight in her father's arms after the fall was much more important than never having fallen at all.

One of the things you learn when you become a father—a sort of realization that starts on the first day and becomes clearer over the years—is that it's not true that you reap what you sow. Sowing is pointless if you don't also set up an irrigation system, keep pests away, pull the weeds, put in stakes until the plants are strong enough to stand on their own. Sowing is pointless if you're not there to pick them up when the wind bends them to the ground.

This holds true for any type of love, but I really only came to understand it this way.

You don't just reap what you sow—that's not true at all. You only reap what you take care of, always.

You Always Laugh

elania has a cough. We were up half the night together—her resting on my chest, me leaning against the headboard a little so her head would be elevated and she would sleep better.

I was awake the whole time listening to her breathe, lost in gloomy thoughts that, as I stroked her hair in the dark, I felt burst like soap bubbles when they get too big. When her breath became slow and regular, I gently freed myself and made a hollow for her between the pillows and Mama, who had taken the first shift that night. I nestled her in, making a little barrier of rolled-up covers on the edge of the bed and went into the kitchen. I made myself a coffee and went down to the studio, since I wasn't going to get any more sleep anyway.

It was 2:14. The computer had been left on and the mailbox notification showed five new messages. I drank my coffee while reading the first three, then Cordelia came into the studio, her nose nodding to the right, the sign that she wanted to go out. I opened the door, we went into the yard, and she ran off. Outside, it seemed like September. I sat down on the wall under the big fir and took a deep breath. The woods were silent, the air was cool but not cold, a dog was barking in the distance. When Cordelia came back, I stood up and went back inside, but passing under the bedroom window, I could hear Melania coughing again. I went upstairs and found her on the bed with her feet where her head should be. I picked her up and pulled her on top of me again, slowly lifted the comforter and covered my feet and her back. We stayed like that for a while.

I had almost fallen back asleep when Ginevra called out. I laid Melania down softly in the hollow and went to check.

"Will you tuck me in?" Ginevra said.

"Of course," I said. "Lie back down."

"Do you know what I dreamed, Daddy?" she said, resting her head on the pillow.

"What?"

"That we were at the beach and you weren't yelling at me anymore."

"Ginevra, I only scold you when you're bad, like yesterday. I don't enjoy yelling at you either, you know that?"

There were a few seconds of silence, which seemed longer in the dark.

"Daddy," she said.

"What is it?" I said.

"When Mommy yells at me, sometimes I'm a little scared. But with you I know you won't do anything."

"That's not true," I said, trying to recover a modicum of paternal authority.

"You always start laughing."

"I start laughing because you're a silly monkey."

"Daddy?"

"What is it?"

"You're laughing, aren't you?"

"Go to sleep," I said, pulling her covers up.

Leaving the room, I paused in the hallway to listen, but Melania wasn't coughing anymore. I went back down to the studio, padding softly down the stairs. I sat down at my table, finished my now cold coffee, picked up a piece of paper, and started drawing. I've been working for five hours, the girls have just woken up, the smile is still there.

Mr. Mbokany

I take the girls to school, then stop by the pediatrician to get a certificate for Melania.

There are seven of us in the waiting room. I'm sitting next to a woman with curly hair gathered at her nape and secretary glasses, typing furiously on her tablet. In front of me there's a black couple with a tiny baby girl whom the mom is nursing; they're so beautiful they look like a painting. A little blond girl with braids, sitting beside a well-dressed grandmother, is watching them, transfixed. When the girl gets down from her seat, the grandma is startled. The girl goes right up to the black couple and before the grandma can stop her she strokes the baby's head. The mom removes the baby girl from her breast, adjusts herself, pats her on the back, and finally sits her on her leg right in front of the girl, as if offering her the baby. The girl stares at them.

"How old are you?" the mother says, in shaky Italian.

"Two," says the girl, holding up two fingers.

"Three now," the grandmother corrected, behind her.

"What's her name?" the girl asks, indicating the baby.

"Her name is Anele," the mother says.

"And how old is she?" the girl says.

"She is two and a half months old," the dad breaks in. "She's a very little baby."

The blond girl reaches close to the baby's face and strokes her once again. The grandma has a look on her face like, "Ebola, here we come." The baby, totally calm, shows a hint of a smile.

"What's her last name?" the girl asks.

"Mbokany," the father says.

The girl tries to say it, but can't get it out.

"It's a hard name," the father says. The blond girl tries again. The pediatrician's door opens.

"Next!" the doctor calls.

The grandma stands up and goes to enter the office.

"Priscilla!" she says when she's almost at the door. "Come on now."

Priscilla doesn't move; she keeps staring at the baby.

"Go on, your mother is calling you," says the black man.

The grandma looks at the man from the door.

"I'm her *grand*-mother," she says, with a note of irritation in her voice.

"Ma'am, I think he meant to pay you a compliment," I say.

The man smiles, the grandmother does not.

"Bokani!" Priscilla says.

"Very good," the man says, "but go with your grandmother now."

Priscilla does as she's told, they go in, the door to the office closes. The man and I exchange glances. The woman with the curly hair continues typing on her tablet.

"It's not that I wanted to compliment her," he says. "It's that in my country grandmother and mother are the same, and even after almost three years I always make that mistake."

"I understand. I said that because calling her 'mother' made her feel younger," I explain.

"*Young* is a compliment?" he says.

"Well, *old* definitely isn't." I laugh.

The man stares at me.

"In our country, elders are the most respected adults, the most precious," he says. "For that reason they were killed in war."

I'm floored, as if someone suddenly turned my head in a different direction.

"But if old people are so precious," I say, "then why are mother and grandmother the same word?"

He gives me a paternal look. I know because I recognize it.

"Because mothers and grandmothers have both given life," he says, indicating first his wife and then his daughter.

I think to myself, this concept is so simple it's wondrous. I look at the man, his poise; listen to his measured, polite speech, not a word out of place. I think how he's there with his family, he brought them here. Whereas I am at the pediatrician's by myself, and the blond girl came with her grandmother, and the curly-haired woman hasn't looked up once since we came in.

I look at him, and I don't know his story; I don't know whether he came here on a rickety old boat or a private jet, if he's a dishwasher or an Oxford graduate. But I can't help but think of that look from Priscilla's grandmother, of the common discussions of "invasion," of those who, without thinking twice, want to "help them in their own country." Of how much we actually need people like this man. To look in different directions. To rediscover the essentials.

To help us a bit in our country.

There's This Mom

There's this mom.

I run into her at the nursery school every morning. I never used to see her. Maybe she changed her schedule, maybe I've started coming earlier. She's a young mom, she comes in leggings and a sweatshirt, straight hair gathered on her head with a blue plastic clip. She always smiles at me. She watches Melania and Ginevra playing, running around by the cubbies, waiting for their turn to enter the kids' room. Then she turns and smiles at me again. She smiles at me every morning.

I never really know how to take it. I don't know whether to take her smile as the smile of a mom or of a woman. It wouldn't make a difference, but that just goes to show that moms and dads live in a bubble that resembles a parallel dimension. The role of parent consumes them almost entirely, to the point where sometimes they even forget they're individuals. Given that I also live and work at home, mine is a bubble with its shutters closed. Inside are Paola and the girls and that's it. I don't need light from outside because the bubble has all the light I need. I think it's like that for a lot of people.

There's this mom. I run into her at the nursery school every morning. I never used to see her. When we see each other I'm often slimy as a squid; my face is haggard from lack of sleep; I wear the only sweat-shirt I've bought in the last six years, perpetually bathed in drool on the left shoulder. She always looks like she just rolled out of bed, she dresses her daughter speaking in hushed tones and carefully fixes her hair. I know her voice, she knows mine, but we've never exchanged a word. I know why not. Because, with what's left of my male vanity, I prefer a woman's smile to a mom's words, or at least like to imagine it. I like to remember.

There's this mom. I run into her at home every morning. Before I met her I'd never seen her. When I'm in the studio working and I hear the bedroom shutters go up, I put my pen down and run up the stairs. If she's back in bed I slide under the covers be-side her; sometimes she's in the bathroom and I wait for her. The first thing she does is ask me about the girls. I tell her everything's fine. When I tell her every-thing's fine she smiles at me softly, with her head on the pillow. Sometimes she just smiles with her eyes.

Her smile is a mother's and a woman's at the same time, and it's all I need.

The Tired Dad

This morning I cross paths with a tired dad.

The tired dad has swollen, red eyes—the left more closed, as if he'd been punched. He hasn't shaved and he has bad breath. He probably didn't sleep well. Maybe he didn't sleep at all. The tired dad grumbles, he has an air about him of "Why do I always have to be the one to take the kids to school?" That look that says "Things were better when they were worse," when women were just mothers and dads left the house at seven in the morning and didn't see them again until eight at night, after a cocktail at the bar. When they came back home and everyone had to be quiet and everything was all ready on the table. Slippers at the door and sometimes a hot bath. When the only conversation with the children before bed was "how was school," and within a few years, it went straight to the fuck-yous and slamming doors. I see the tired dad linger. His eyes are vacant. You can tell his mind is occupied by work, money, problems. He looks around as if searching for an escape. The morning light coming in through the window is a promise that doesn't mean anything to him. The tired dad thinks—I'm sure—that things will change, that really it's just a phase, that the kids will grow up and slowly become more independent and he'll be free again, even from his worries. But instead today's worries will be replaced by tomorrow's, which won't be better or worse, just different. He won't be ready then either. Tomorrow he'll still have to make do with what he's got, thinking, "If only they'd told me before . . ." They did tell you, earlier. But knowing beforehand doesn't prepare you. Knowing beforehand doesn't help anything. The tired dad takes a deep breath, runs a hand through his thinning hair, coughs as if to clear his throat, and says to himself, "Let's go." He stops staring at the mirror, puts on a nice smile, and goes to wake them up for school.

When Ginevra jumps into my arms in the dark without even looking, the tiredness slips away like water off goose feathers.

The Day

Today is the day.

We're finally giving it a try. For the first time since Melania was born we're leaving her at Grandma and Grandpa Bussola's for the whole afternoon. Yes, her, the one who, when she sees other human beings over eight years old who aren't Mommy, Daddy, or the grandparents who've already been approved, screams so loud you could use it as a foghorn across the Bering Strait. To make the situation easier, we're also leaving Virginia, who is one of the people she trusts. My father has already dusted off his collection of turn-of-the-century nursery rhymes in dialect; my mother already worried that Melania wouldn't eat, so she went shopping three weeks ago and asked me "What if I make . . . ?" So as not to offend her, I don't say that all she needs is a bag of stale chips, that to bribe Melania, all it takes is a chocolate-dipped mini Magnum bar, and without one, forget it. Paola started getting anxious at the end of August. Last year.

Everything's been planned down to the smallest detail. We will arrive at Grandma and Grandpa Busso-la's around 2:30 to 3:00 p.m., just to break up their afternoon nap and take them when they're already at a high level of sociability. We will spend an hour sitting on the couch with Melania stuck to me like a mussel on a rock, her head buried in the crook of my neck, my father an inch away, blowing out my right eardrum with a little wooden bell from 1948, repeating "It's Grandpa! It's Grandpa!" at the back of Melania's neck. Paola will amiably occupy my mother on their favorite subject: meteorology. Today they are supposed to discuss the details of "Babson's Barometric Curve: The Rainfall of Fall 2015 Compared with That of Spring 1982." The other two daughters will try to provide ambience by making a cheerful domestic atmosphere: Virginia will show them "the tallest tower in the world" with Lego blocks, Ginevra will do an ice routine dressed as Elsa from *Frozen* using a Kinder Bueno candy bar from Grandma's secret stash as a magic wand. Around 4:00 I'll try to get up from the couch nonchalantly, will gently pass Melania to Mama, and we'll trade places. Paola will sit on the couch with her while my father temporarily blinds her, spinning his 1956 brass kaleidoscope in the air and singing "It's Grandpa! It's Grandpa!" My mother and I will resume our favorite subject: "An Introduction to Fiscal Phenomenology," alternating with the ever relevant: "Have you paid the car registration?"

Around 5:00 my father will offer us some of his garlic toast as a courtesy, Paola will graciously decline because otherwise, so as not to offend him, she would have to eat a whole tray of it, washed down with "this pleasant, smooth red that is only 19 percent alcohol." And it will be there, right in that moment, while my mind's clouded by the fumes of alcohol, that we'll subtly make our escape. Paola will give Melania a little kiss on the forehead, trying to peel her from my leg; Virginia will turn on cartoons for her, putting on the episode of *Peppa Pig* where George has the hiccups; Ginevra will take off her Elsa dress and put on her Rapunzel travel dress. My mother will look at me with bloodshot and falsely calm eyes saying, "Don't worry, for goodness' sake, it's just a baby!" while clutching a screaming Melania who's bursting her left eardrum and also losing use of her right eardrum as my father shakes his handcrafted beech wood maracas from 1972 filled with river pebbles and bullet shells and yells: "It's Grandpa! It's Grandpa!"

We will ride off into the dim light of sunset, with only Rapunzel in the backseat; she can barely contain the joy of being an only child for a night. We'll get to our 6:30 appointment in the city late because, well, you try to find parking in the city on a Saturday. We won't even make it to the bend in the road before the phone rings. I will answer without even looking at the number. It'll be my mother asking me, "Well, what if

I make . . . ?" and in the background a merchant ship in the fog of the Bering Strait, the *Peppa* episode with the wasp on Papa Pig's cake, all tied together with the notes of a 1973 barrel organ and my father singing "It's Grandpa! It's Grandpa!" to the tune of the socialist "Internationale."

Two of Hearts

Every morning I help Ginevra wash her face.

While I wash it, I sing. So I've done since she was born. Silly little songs we've made up ourselves, featuring slimy little noses and crusty little eyes.

Today, as I wipe her face with water, Ginevra said commandingly: "No more singing, Daddy!"

I asked why.

"Because now that I'm big I don't like it anymore."

Yesterday, Virginia returned from her first sleepover at the house of a friend from school. She arrived at ten in the morning with the earbuds of her iPod buried in her ears and climbed out of the car of other parents who, to me, were nobody except people other than me. She told me how she slept in the basement with three of her friends on a giant sofa bed and had stayed up past midnight.

Melania has learned to say "ciao." She used to say "tao" or "ao," but most of the time she seemed to stumble into the word by pure chance without really understanding what it meant. Whereas now she looks you in the eyes and says *"ciaooo,"* then runs off as if she were going to miss her bus.

The first signs, orbits growing wider, little things that change forever.

In a poem, Kahlil Gibran said parents are like bows from which, like living arrows, children are sent forward.

What Gibran doesn't say is that each child is a double-headed arrow. When you shoot it, the first arrowhead flies away from you, following its trajectory into a future that isn't yours. The second, meanwhile, shoots backward and sticks forever in your chest. To remind you that you remain archers even without your arrows; the pain you felt looming over you like an omen from the first day will be there to stay and will mark out the rest of your life.

Every father and every mother are united by a wound that never closes up.

That wound is even stronger than the love that united them and unites them still. It's what transformed them from lovers into archers, from partners to veterans. And that irremovable arrowhead is what will always allow their hearts, despite everything, to go on beating as one.